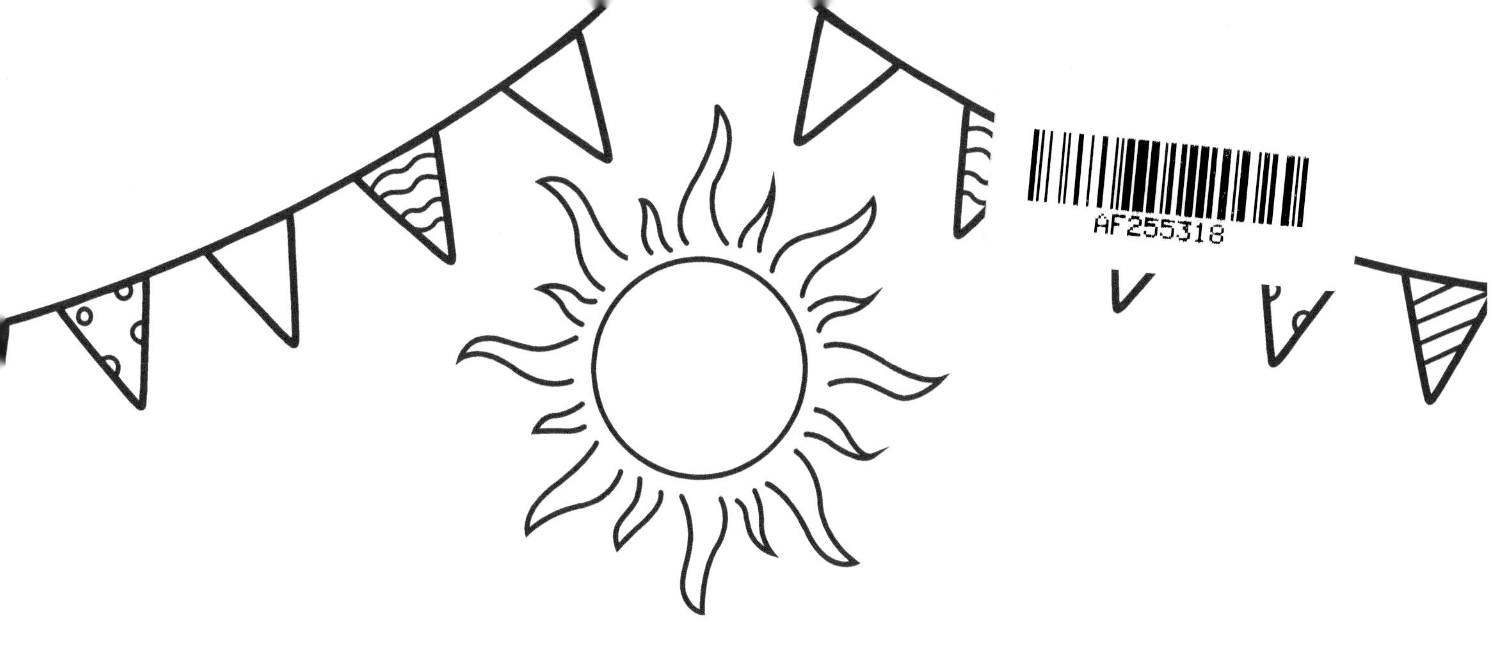

# This Journal Belongs to the

## Family

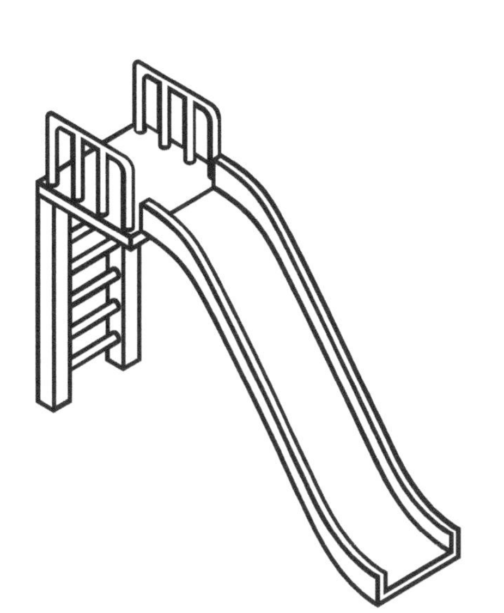

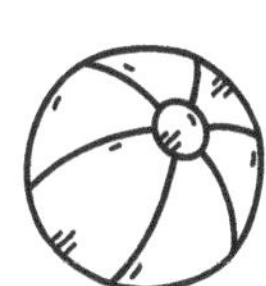

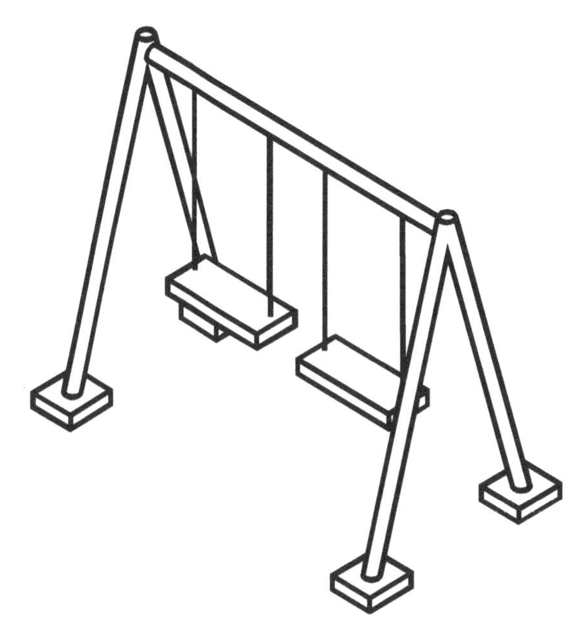

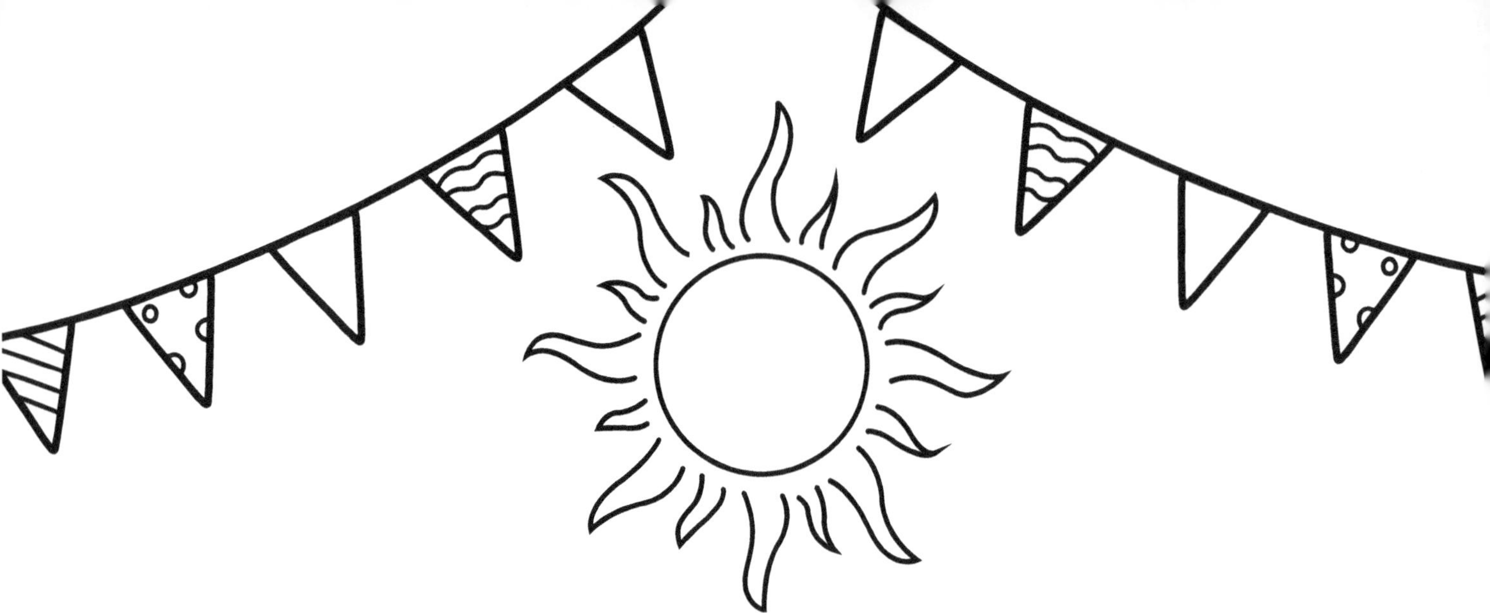

Thank you for purchasing 'Our Playground Photo Journal'.

This journal includes photo challenges and 'get to know you' questions that will help collect memories of your family's park and playground adventures, connect, and explore your child's perspective of life.

The pages have been left white for your child to be the artist who brings the drawings to life, with pencil and crayon!

Inclusive play equipment allows children of all ages, abilities, cultures, and backgrounds to play next to, alongside, and with each other, fostering greater acceptance and friendships. As you visit each playground and complete challenges, consider who could access that equipment and if they cannot, what we can do in future updates to ensure it is as inclusive as possible.

I hope that you enjoy using this journal with your family and share the love with others.

If you are on Instagram, please like and follow Berry Bee Publishing and use the hashtag #OurPlaygroundPhotoJournal when you complete each photo challenge!

From my family to yours, enjoy!

# Contents Page

Berry Bee Publishing
Perth, Western Australia
Author © 2024 Michelle De Robillard
Illustrations © 2024 Canva.com



Softcover - 9 780 645 959 949

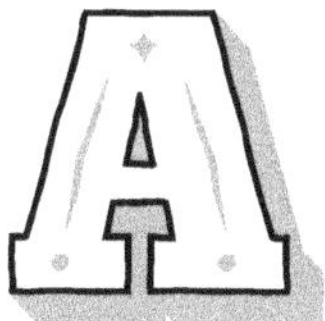

**Challenge**:
Take a photo of your child at a playground/park with a name or in a suburb beginning with the letter A.

Date:                              Location:

Today's
weather
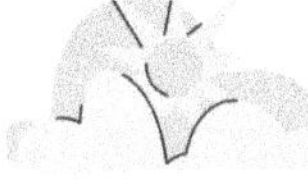 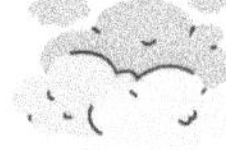 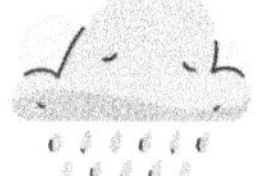 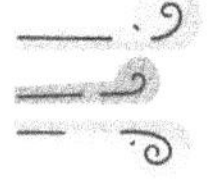 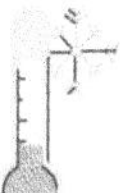

How many
people?
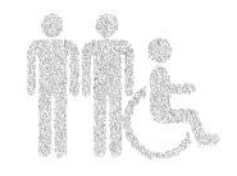 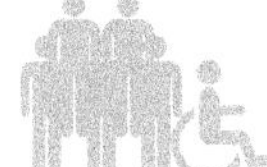 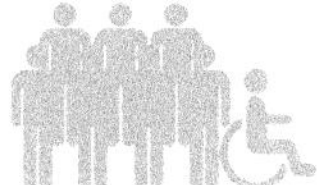 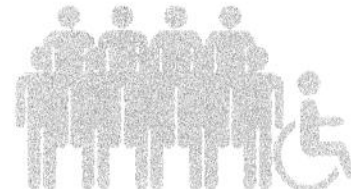

What is your favourite part of the playground?


Would you prefer to go on a swing or down a slide? Why?


How many different types of animals can you see at this playground?

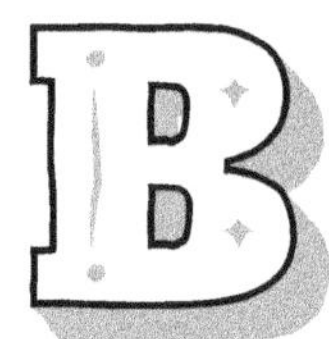



**Challenge:**
Take a photo of your child at a playground/park with a name or in a suburb beginning with the letter B.

Date:                                  Location:

Today's
weather
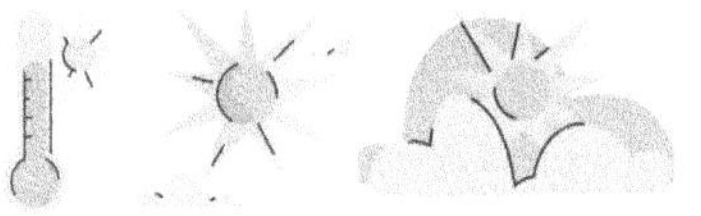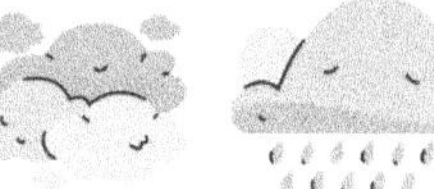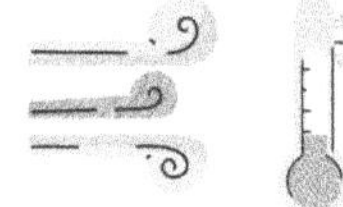

How many
people?
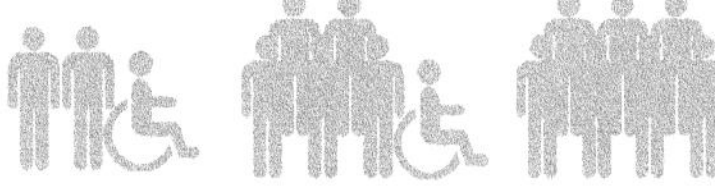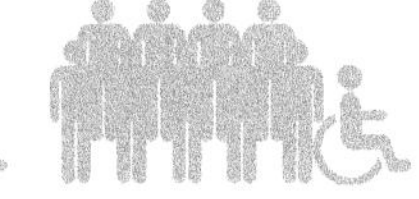

What is your favourite thing to bring to the playground?


Would you rather be a butterfly or a bee? Why?


If you could have breakfast at dinner time or dinner at breakfast time, which would you choose?

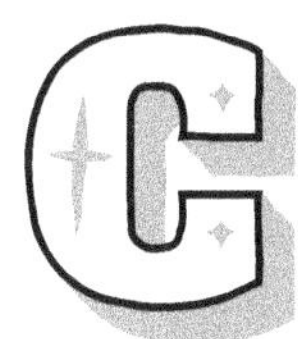

**Challenge:**
Take a photo of your child at a playground/park with a name or in a suburb beginning with the letter C.

Date:                          Location:

Today's
weather     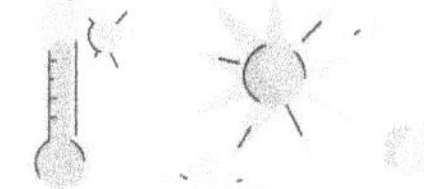 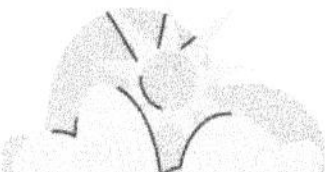 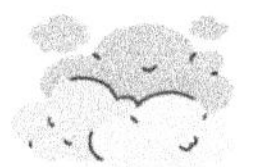 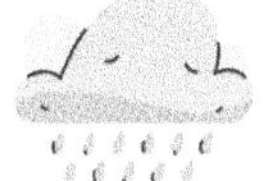 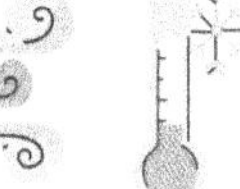

How many
people?     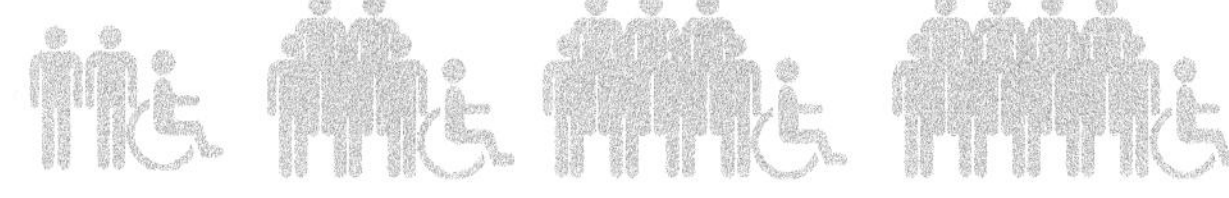

Do you like going to the park more when it is sunny or cloudy?

What made you smile today?

If you could be a cat at a playground, what would you do?

# D

**Challenge:**
Take a photo of your child at a playground/park with a name or in a suburb beginning with the letter D.

Date:                              Location:

Today's
weather

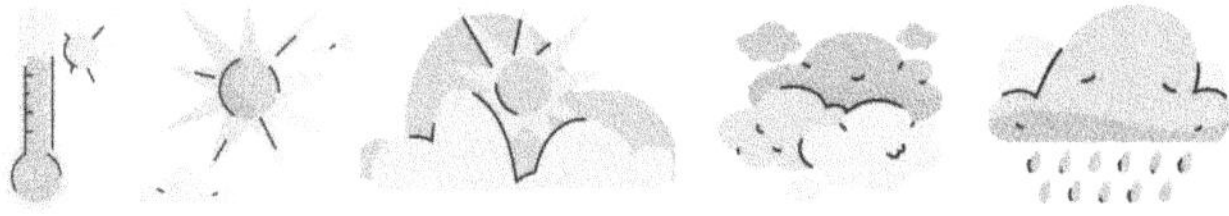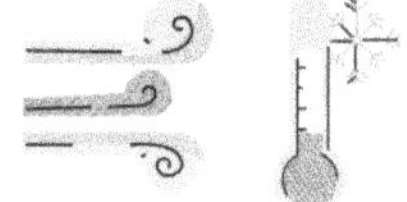

How many
people?

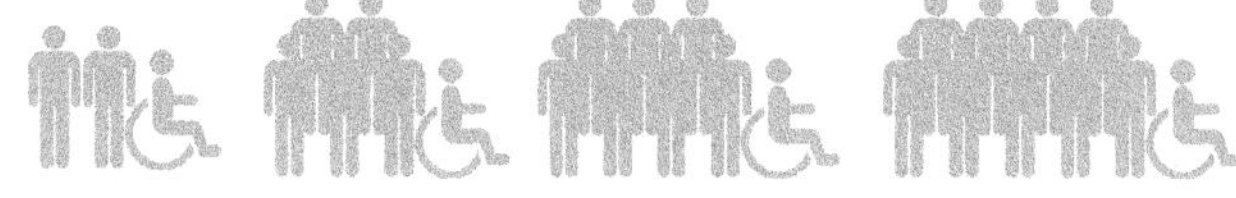

Would you rather be a duck or a dog? Why?

What was your dad's favourite part of a playground when he was a child?

If you could draw your dream playground, what would it include?

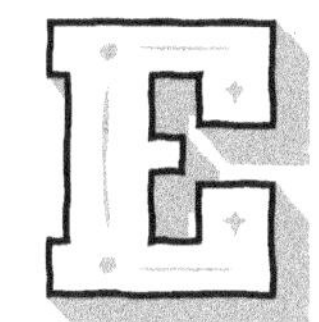

**Challenge:**
Take a photo of your child at a playground/park with a name or in a suburb beginning with the letter E.

Date:                              Location:

Today's
weather     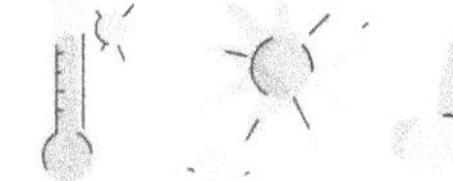 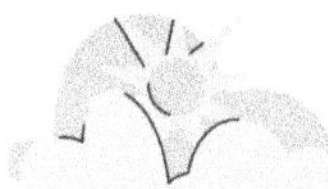 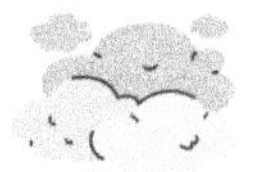 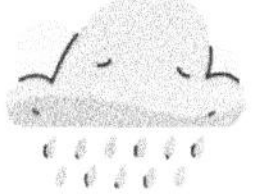 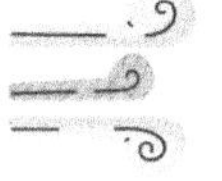 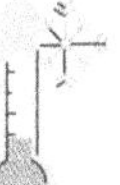

How many
people?     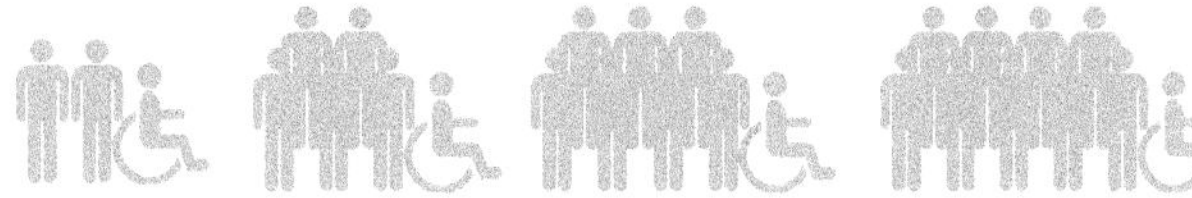

Would you rather fly like an eagle or be as big as an elephant?

How many entry's and exit's does the playground and park have?

What did you find easy to do at the playground? What did you find hard to do?

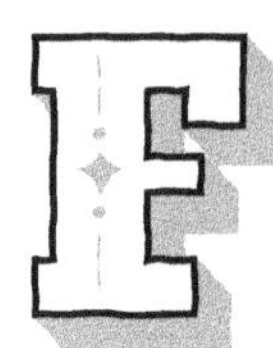

**Challenge:**
Take a photo of your child at a playground/park with a name or in a suburb beginning with the letter F.

Date:                              Location:

Today's
weather

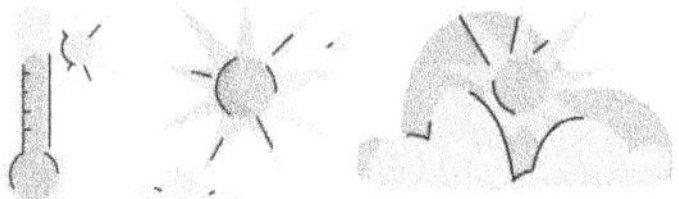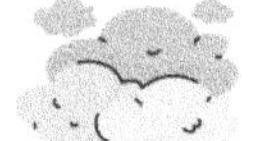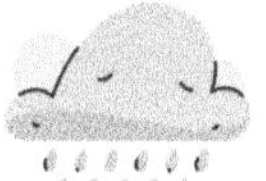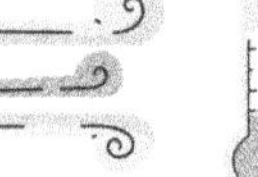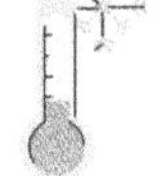

How many
people?

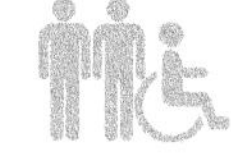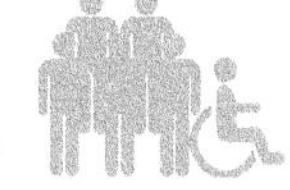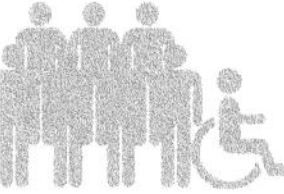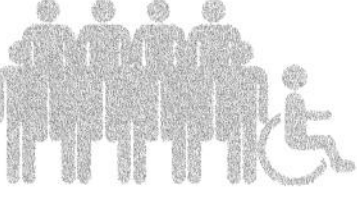

Would you rather go on a flying fox or play in a fountain?

Who is your favourite friend to play with at a playground?

Find and list all the things at the park starting with the letter F?

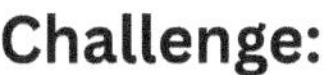



**Challenge:**
Take a photo of your child at a playground/park with a name or in a suburb beginning with the letter G.

Date:                                    Location:

Today's
weather
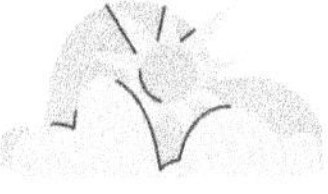 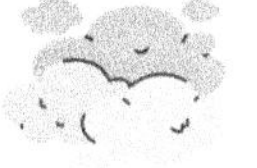 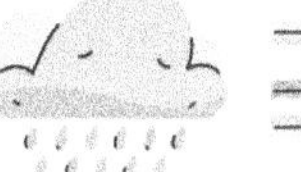 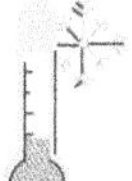

How many
people?
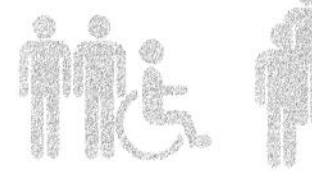 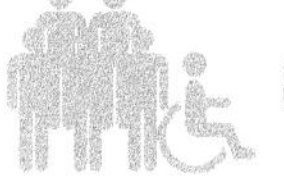 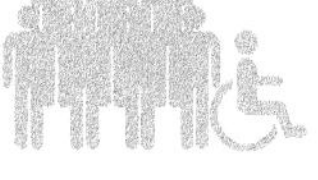 

What made you giggle at this playground?


Would you rather be a gorilla or a giraffe?


What did your grandmother and/or grandfather love to play on as a child?

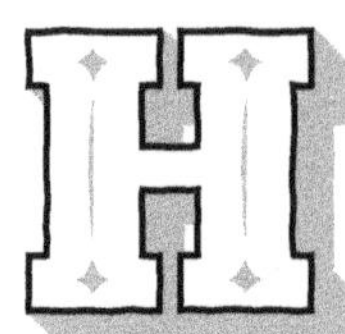

**Challenge:**
Take a photo of your child at a playground/park with a name or in a suburb beginning with the letter H.

Date:                              Location:

Today's
weather

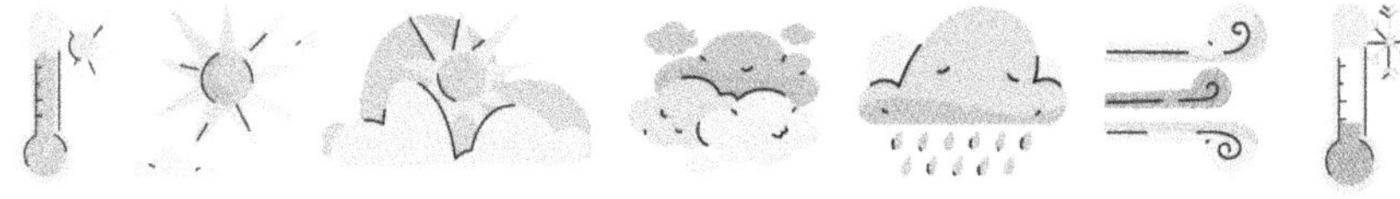

How many
people?

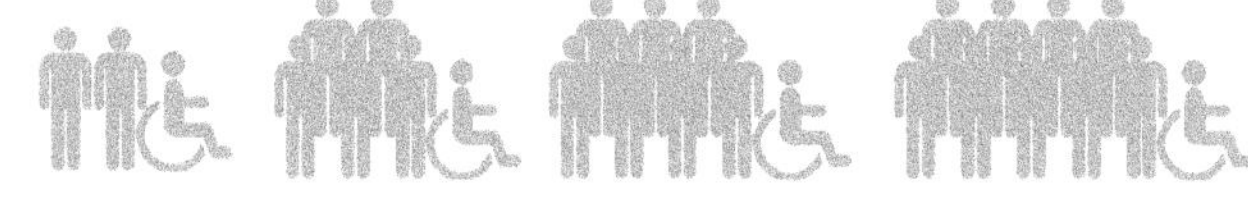

How do you help your friends when at a playground/park?




Who is your favourite super-hero? Why?




Would you rather be a horse or a hyena? Why?

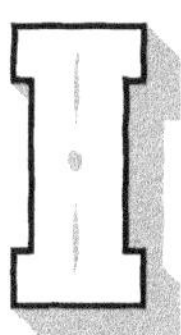

**Challenge:**
Take a photo of your child at a playground/park with a name or in a suburb beginning with the letter I.

Date:                                    Location:

Today's
weather

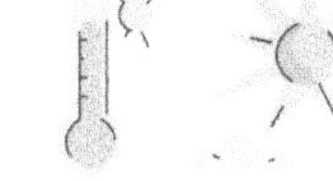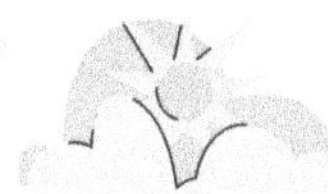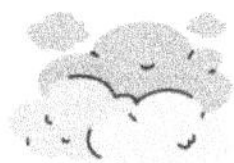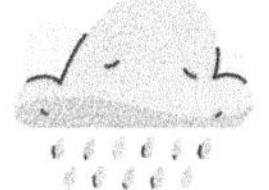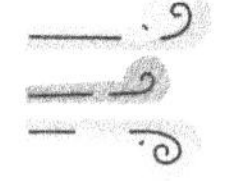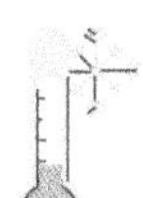

How many
people?

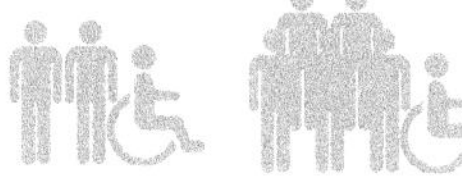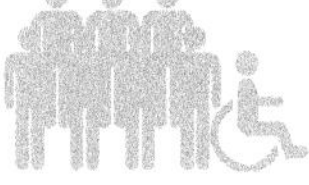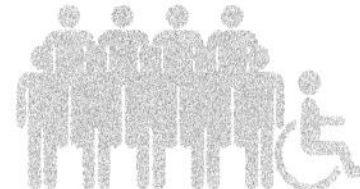

How can you include other children in your play?

Would you rather live in an igloo or on an iceberg?

What can you climb into at this playground?

## Challenge:
Take a photo of your child at a playground/park with a name or in a suburb beginning with the letter J.

Date:                          Location:

Today's
weather
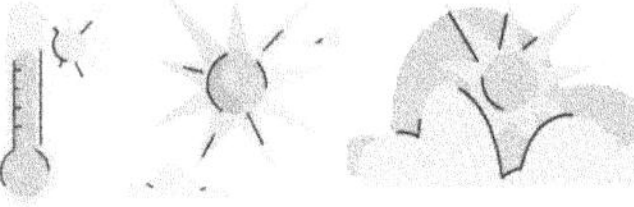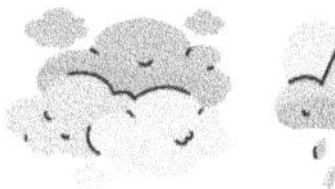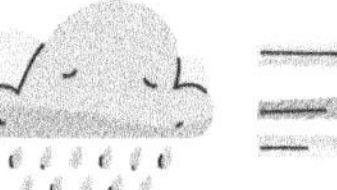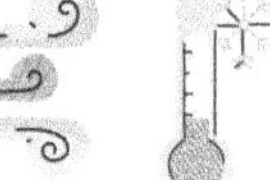

How many
people?
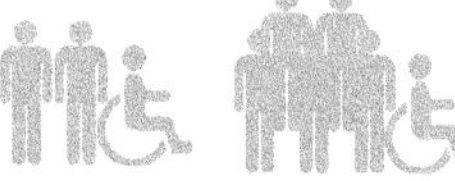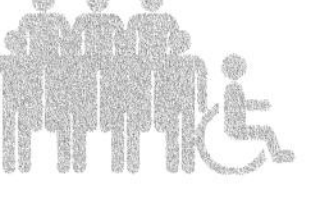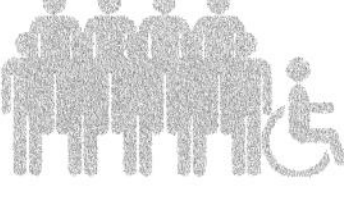

Where in the playground do you feel the most joy?


If you could be a jellyfish or a jaguar, what would you be?


What is your favourite part of the playground to jump on?

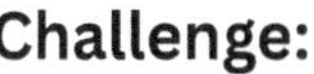



Date:                              Location:

Today's
weather

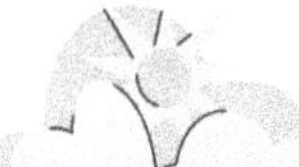 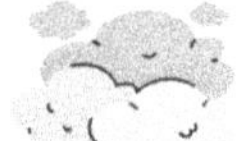 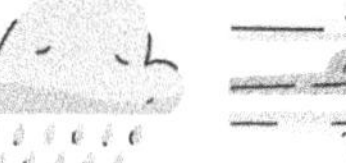 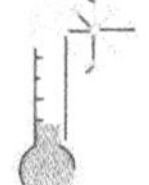

How many
people?

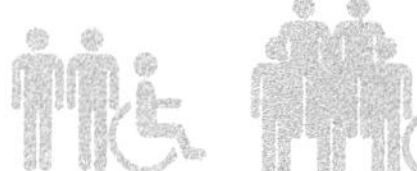 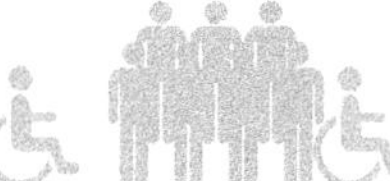 

How do you show kindness to a new friend at the playground?

Would you rather kick a ball or do karate?

If you could be a kangaroo or a koala, what would you be?

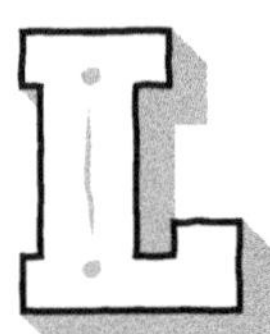

**Challenge:**
Take a photo of your child at a playground/park with a name or in a suburb beginning with the letter L.

Date:                          Location:

Today's weather 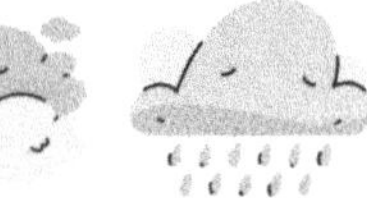 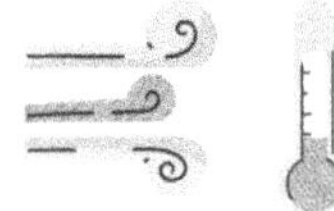

How many people? 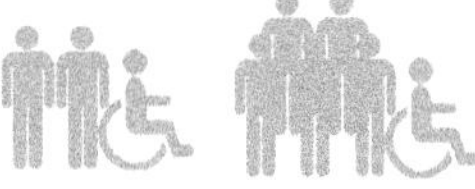 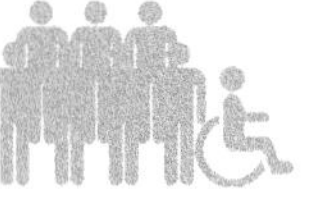 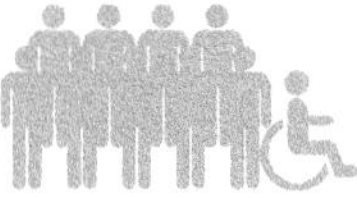

What made you laugh at the playground today?

Would you rather be a lion or a lizard?

How many ladders are there in the playground?

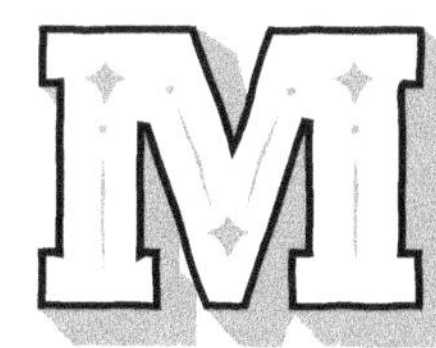



**Challenge:**
Take a photo of your child at a playground/park with a name or in a suburb
beginning with the letter M.

Date:                              Location:

Today's
weather 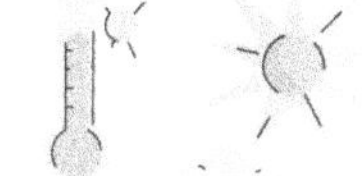 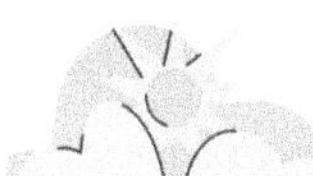 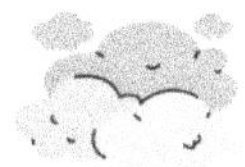 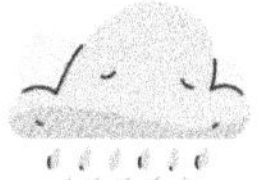 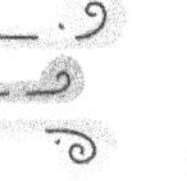 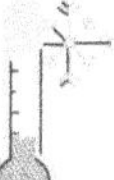

How many
people? 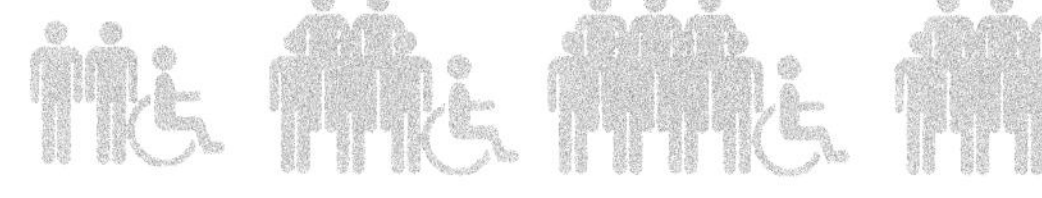

Do you prefer to play on the monkey bars or the merry-go-round at a
playground?


What was your mum's favourite part of a playground when she was a child?


Would you rather be a monkey or a manta ray? Why?

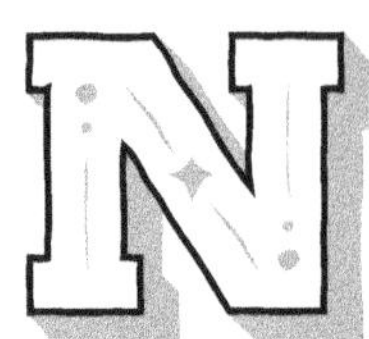

**Challenge:**
Take a photo of your child at a playground/park with a name or in a suburb beginning with the letter N.

Date:                              Location:

Today's
weather

How many
people?

What made you feel silly and fun at this playground?

If you could be a narwhal or a nightingale, what would you be?

How many nocturnal (comes out at night) animals do you know?

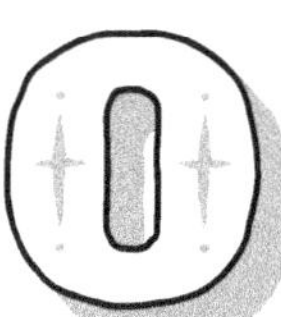



**Challenge:**
Take a photo of your child at a playground/park with a name or in a suburb beginning with the letter O.

Date:                               Location:

Today's
 weather
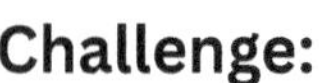

How many
people?

How many things at the playground can open and shut?


Would you rather be an otter or an octopus? Why?


What is your favourite thing to do when outside?

# P

**Challenge:**
Take a photo of your child at a playground/park with a name or in a suburb beginning with the letter P.

Date:                              Location:

Today's
weather
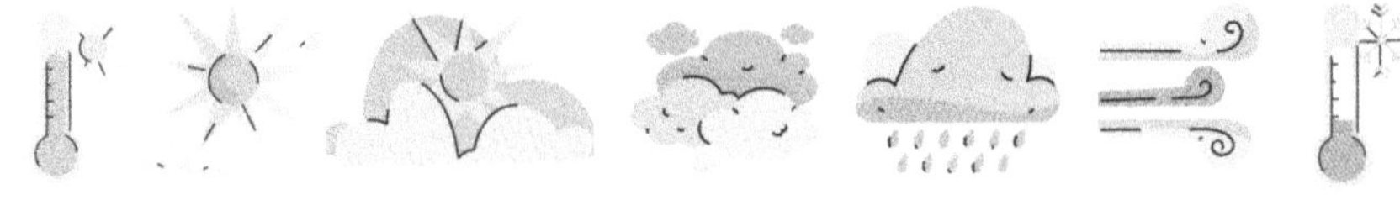

How many
people?
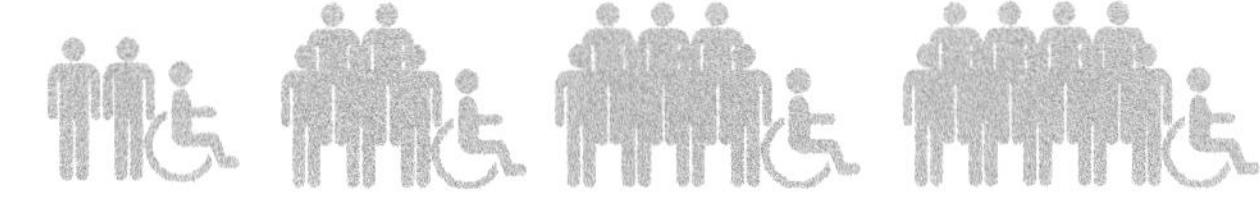

Who was your favourite person to play with today?


Find something pretty to give to your parent. What was it?


What is your favourite thing to paint?

**Challenge:**
Take a photo of your child at a playground/park with a name or in a suburb beginning with the letter Q.

Date:                                    Location:

Today's
 weather      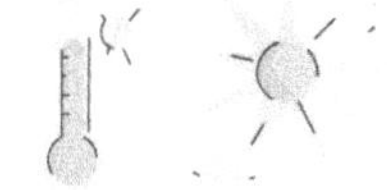 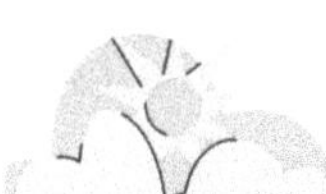 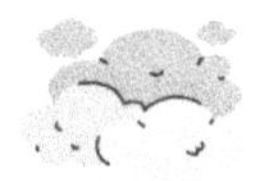 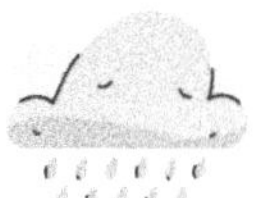 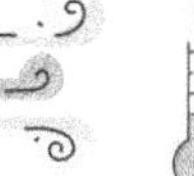

How many
people?      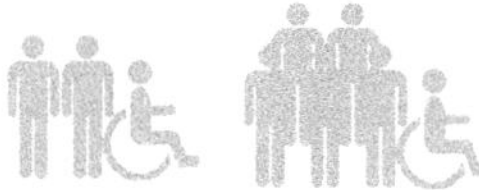 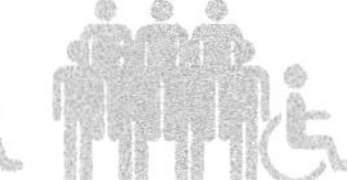 

What was your favoruite quiet place at this playground?

Do you prefer to play quietly or really loudly at the playground?

Would you rather be on a beach like a quokka or in the grass like a quail?

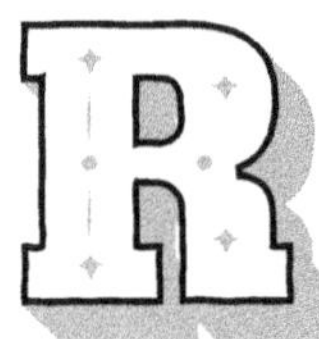

## Challenge:

Take a photo of your child at a playground/park with a name or in a suburb beginning with the letter R.

Date:                              Location:

Today's
weather

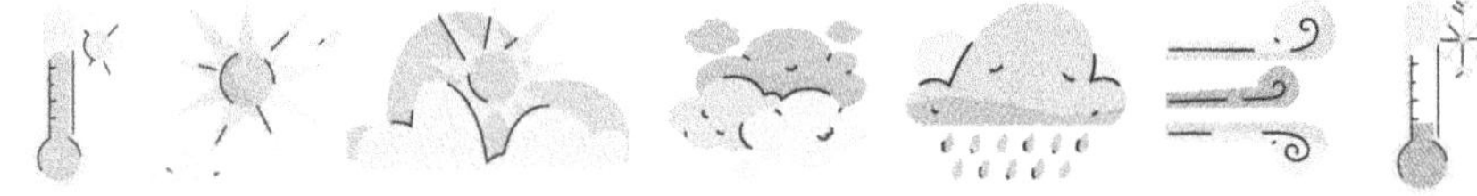

How many
people?

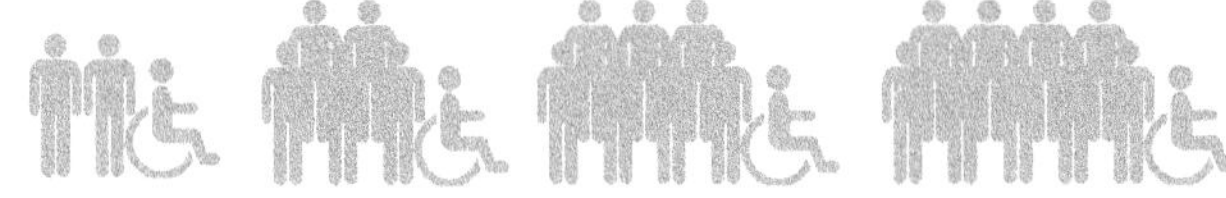

If you could be a rhinoceros or a raccoon, which would you be?

How do you stay safe when near a road or car park?

Would you rather run a race or run up a ramp?

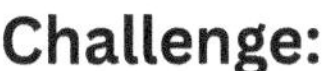



**Challenge:**
Take a photo of your child at a playground/park with a name or in a suburb beginning with the letter S.

Date:                               Location:

Today's weather

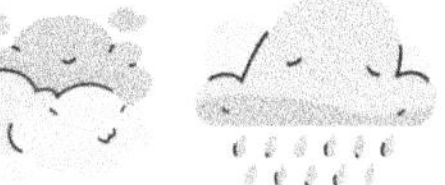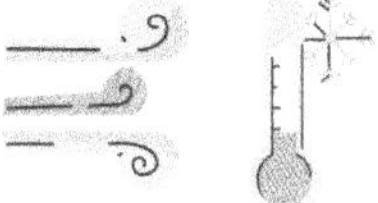

How many people?

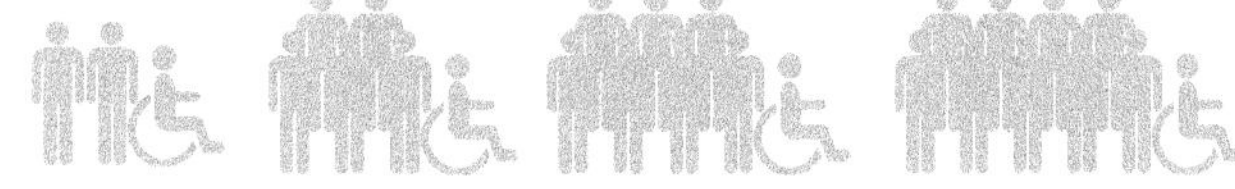

What do you bring to the playground to be sun smart?

What would you do if you saw a snake, skunk or spider near the playground?

What things at the park begin with the letter 'S'?

**Challenge:**
Take a photo of your child at a playground/park with a name or in a suburb beginning with the letter T.

Date:                          Location:

Today's
weather

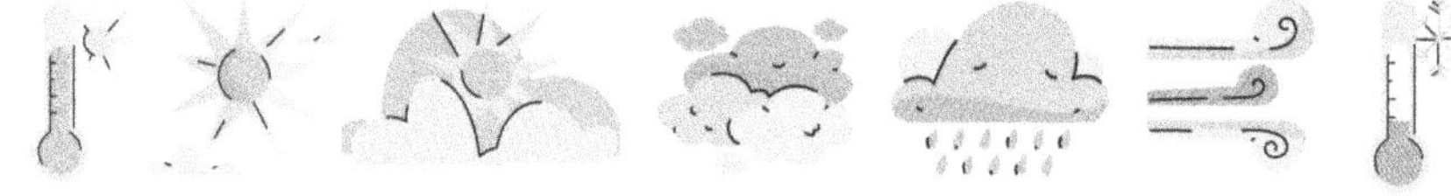

How many
people?

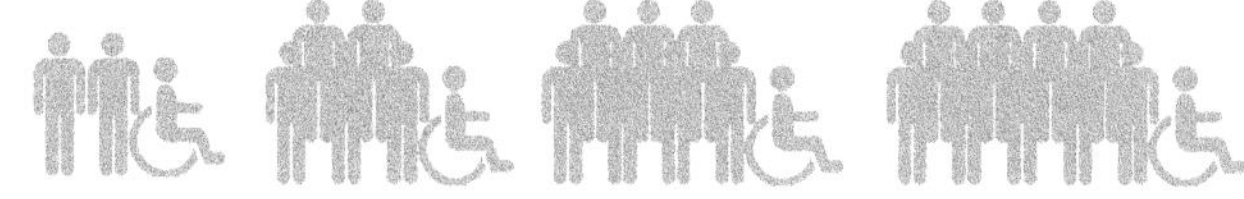

Do you think your teacher would like this playground? What would they like?

What is your favourite thing to take to the park with you?

Would you rather be a tiger or a turtle? Why?

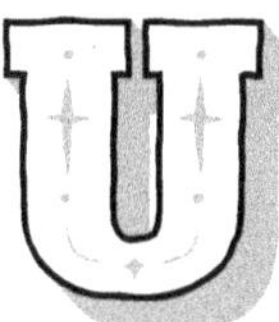



**Challenge:**
Take a photo of your child at a playground/park with a name or in a suburb beginning with the letter U.

Date:                              Location:

Today's
weather
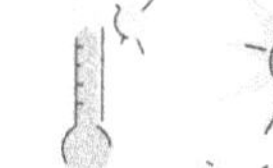 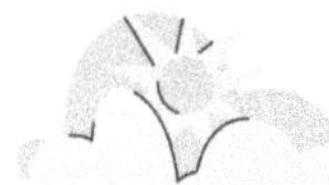 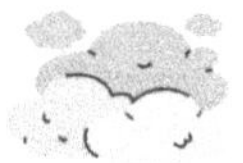 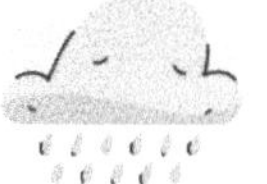 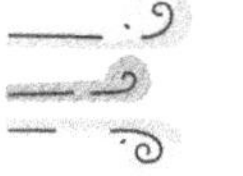 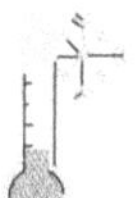

How many
people?
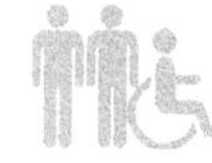 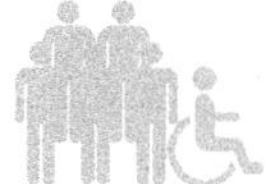 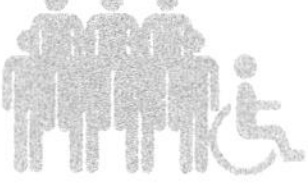 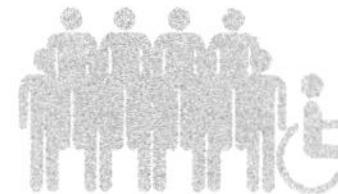

If you had a pet unicorn, what would you name it? Where would you ride it?

What is your Uncle's favourite part of a playground from when he was a child?

Would you rather go for a fly in a UFO or learn to ride a unicycle?

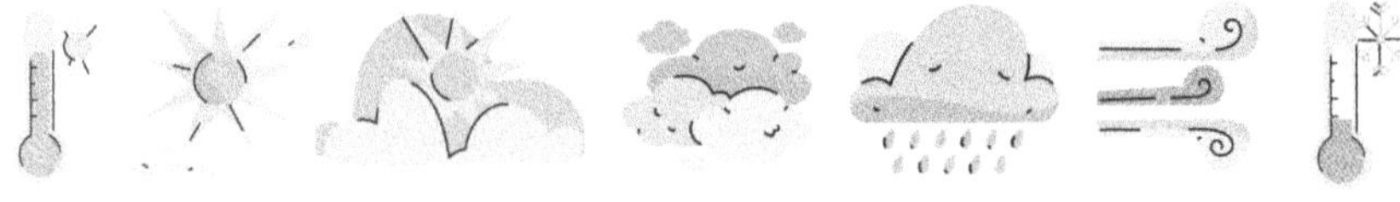

**Challenge:**
Take a photo of your child at a playground/park with a name or in a suburb beginning with the letter V.

Date:                    Location:

Today's
weather

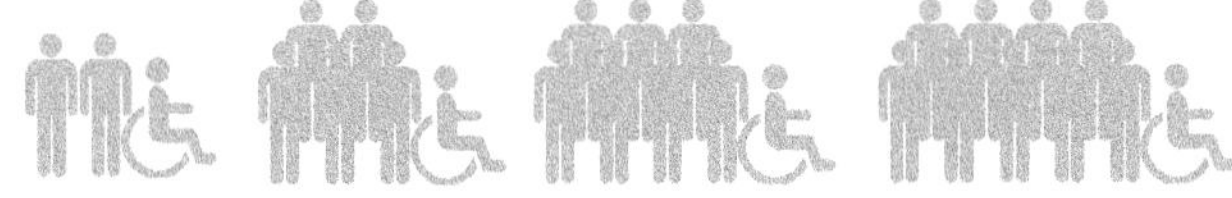

How many
people?

If you could come to this park everyday, what would you do?

Would you rather be a vulture or a vampire bat?

What would you do if you saw a van or other car following you?

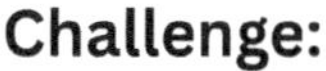



**Challenge:**
Take a photo of your child at a playground/park with a name or in a suburb beginning with the letter W.

Date:                    Location:

Today's
weather

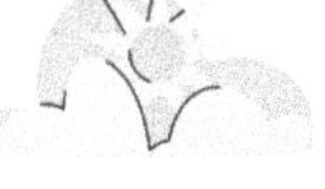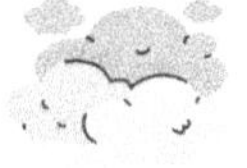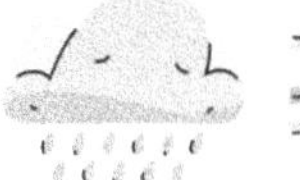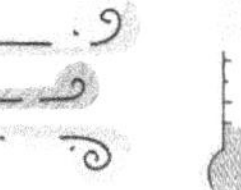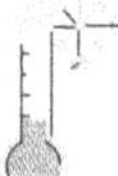

How many
people?

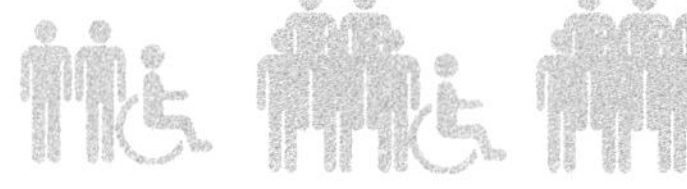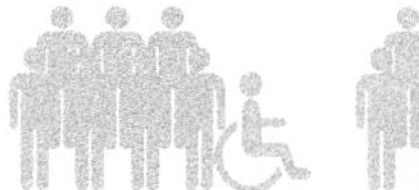

Would you visit this playground again if you could?

How many wheels can you see at this playground?

What can you see in the playground that is made from wood?

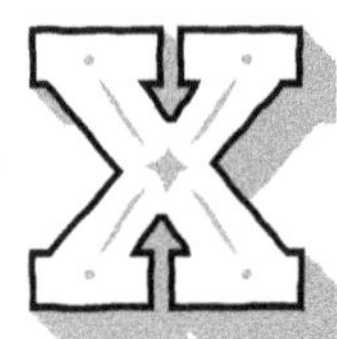



**Challenge:**
Take a photo of your child at a playground/park with a name or in a suburb beginning with the letter X.

Date:                                    Location:

Today's
weather

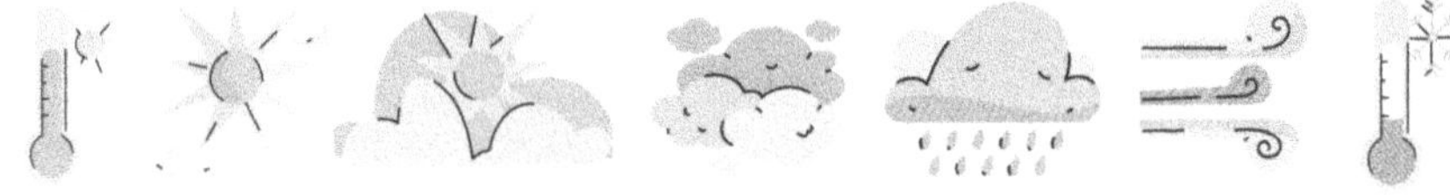

How many
people?

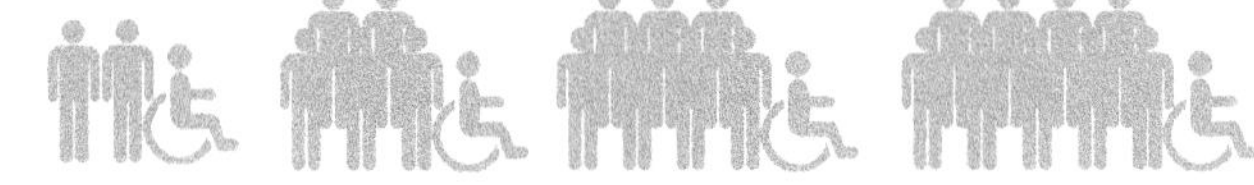

What was your favourite activity today?

How many musical instruments, like a xylophone, can you name?

X marks the spot for a pirate's treasure! If you were a pirate at this playground, where would you hide your treasure?

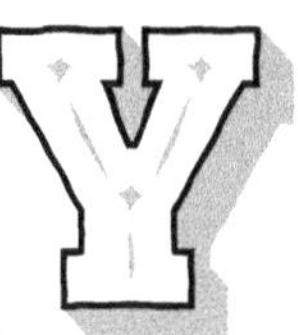

**Challenge:**
Take a photo of your child at a playground/park with a name or in a suburb beginning with the letter Y.

Date:                              Location:

Today's
weather          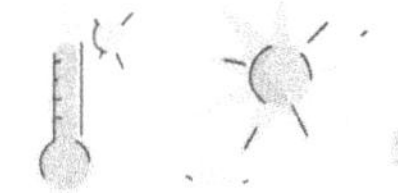 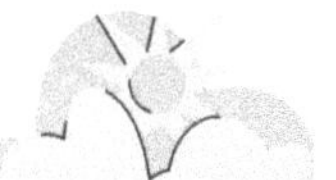 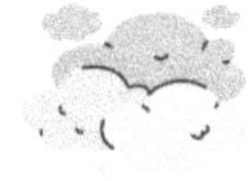 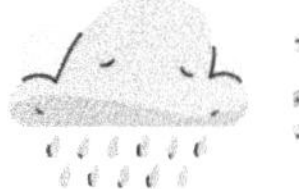 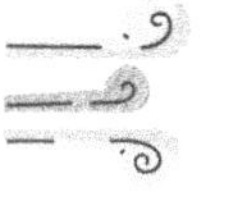 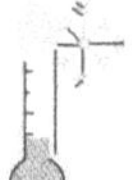

How many
people?          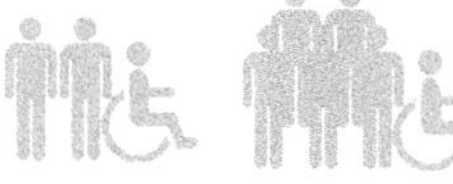 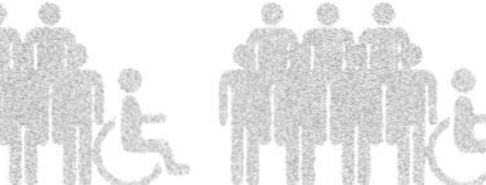 

Would you rather have a ride on a yak or on a yacht?

What was your favourite playground equipment at this playground?

If you could never yawn or yell again, what would you pick?

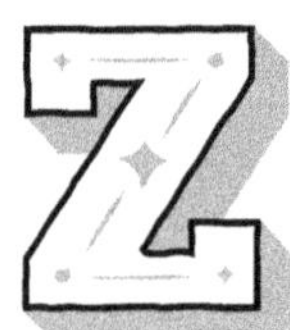

**Challenge:**
Take a photo of your child at a playground/park with a name or in a suburb beginning with the letter Z.

Date:                              Location:

Today's
weather 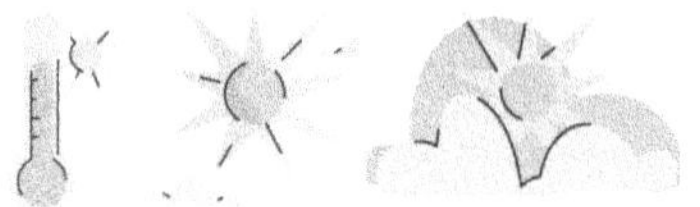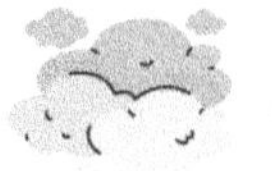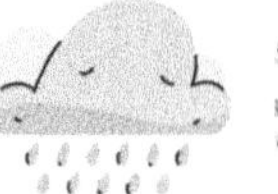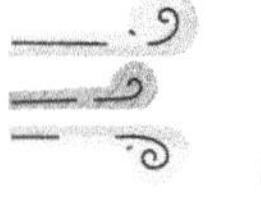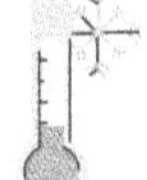

How many
people? 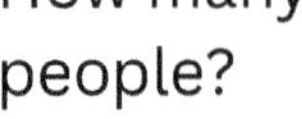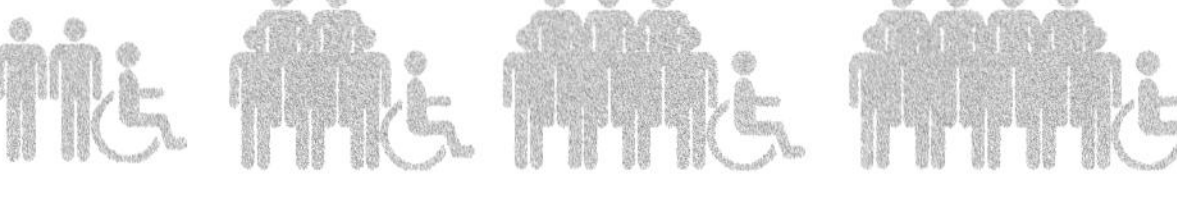

Would you want to come back to this playground? Why?


If you could be a zebra or a zoo keeper, what would you be?


What do you do at a zebra crossing to stay safe?

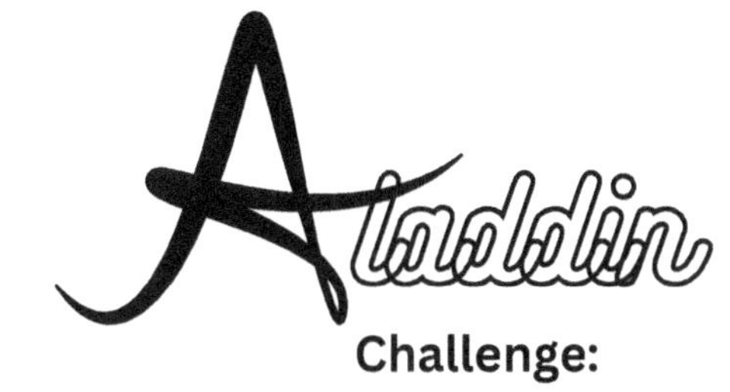 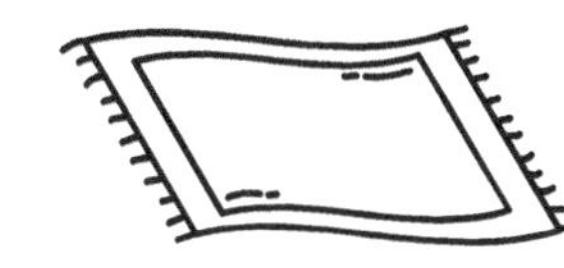

**Challenge:**
Take a photo of your child on a slide on their
magic carpet (a jumper)?

Date:                    Location:

Today's
weather     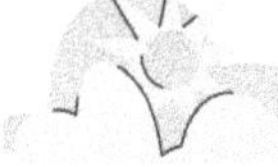 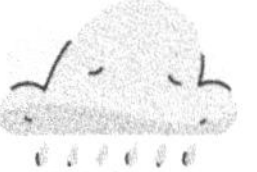 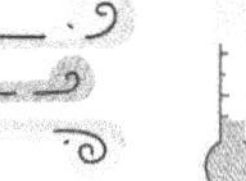 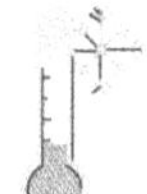

How many
people?     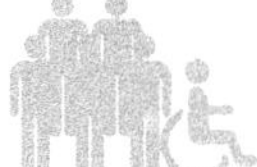 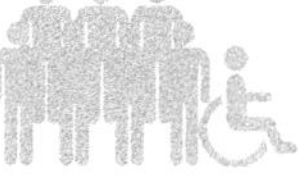 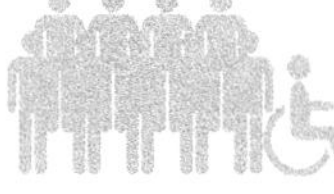

If you could have three wishes, what would they be?

Where would you go if you had a magic carpet?

Would you rather have a pet tiger or a pet monkey?

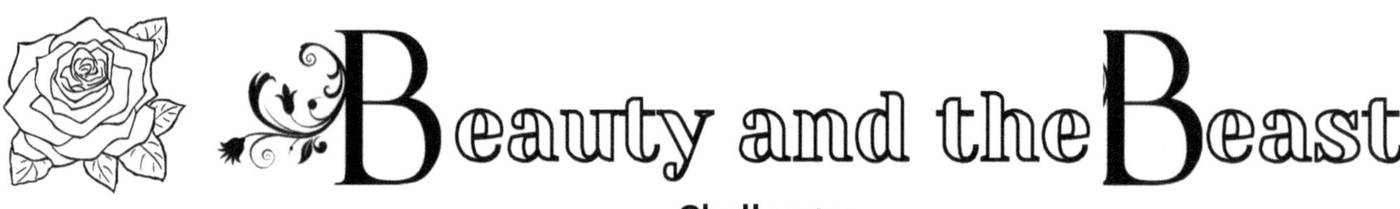


**Challenge:**
Take a photo of your child with their favourite flower
at the playground/park.

Date:                    Location:

Today's
weather 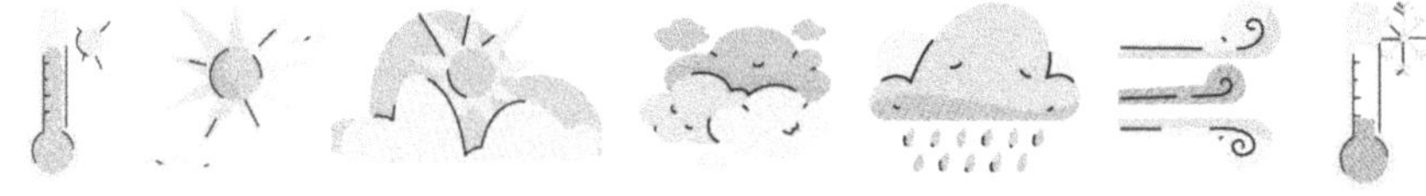

How many
people? 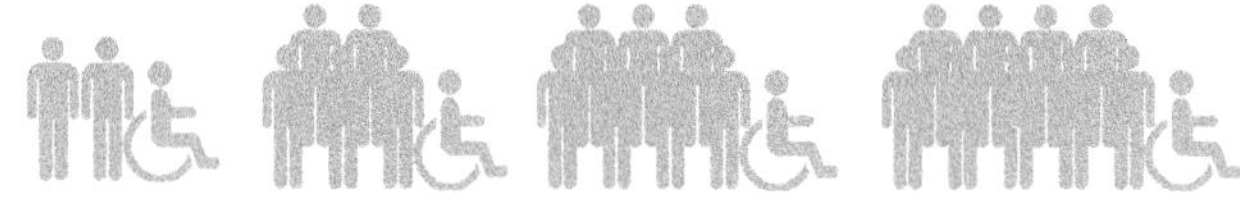

If your were the Beast, where would your castle be?


At the library, where is your favourite place to sit?


What is your favourite book to read at home?

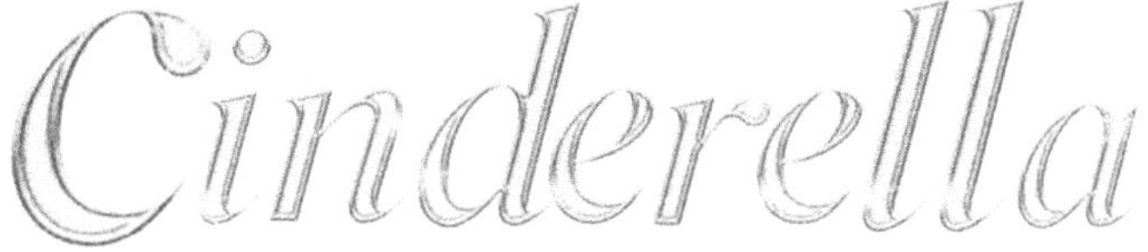 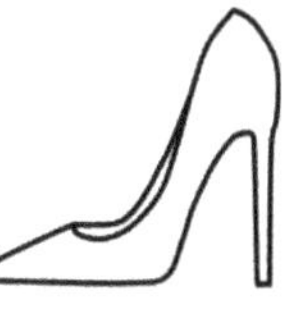

# Cinderella

**Challenge:**
Take a photo of your child at the bottom of a staircase/ladder
with their shoe above them.

Date:                              Location:

Today's
weather

How many
people?

How clean is the park/playground? Do you think it could be cleaner?

If you had a fairy godparent, what wish would you ask them to grant?

When you are cleaning at home, what is your favourite song to listen to?

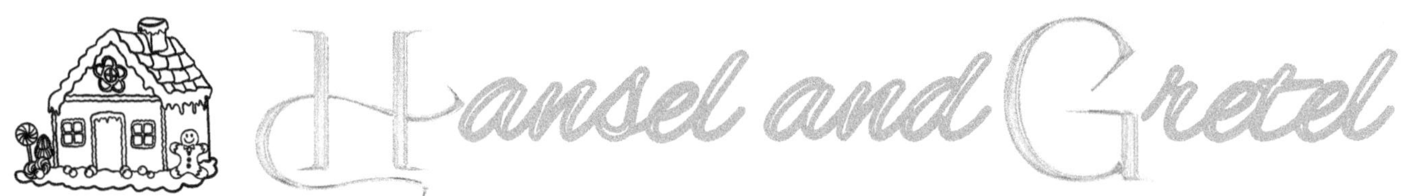

# Hansel and Gretel

**Challenge:**
Take a photo of your child eating a candy or lolly in front
of a cubby house/store.

Date:                                      Location:

Today's
weather
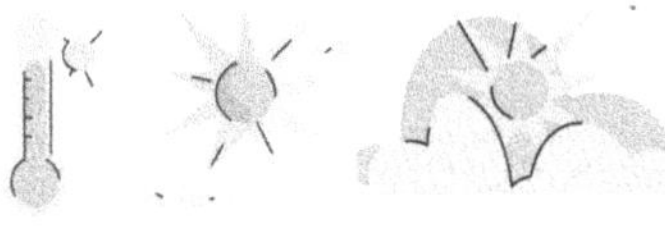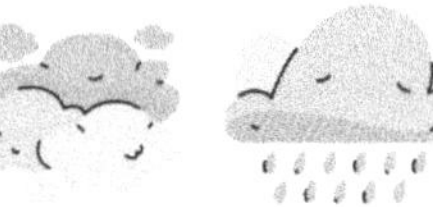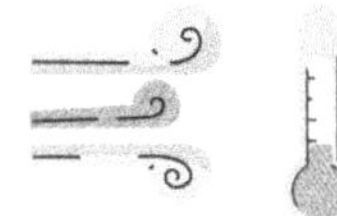

How many
people?
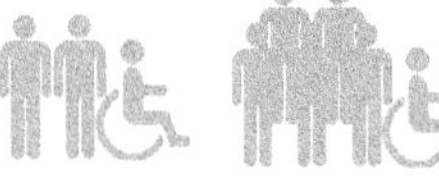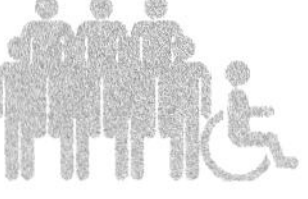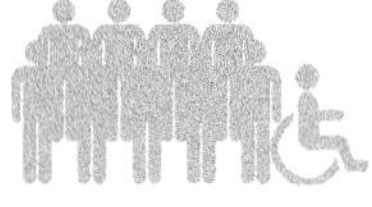

What is your favourite type of sweet food to eat?


Where is your favourite forest or bush to walk in?


If you could not find a parent, what would you do? Where would you go?

# 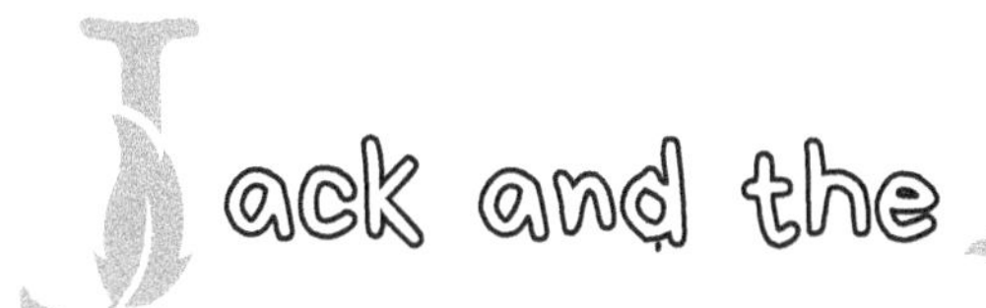ack and the 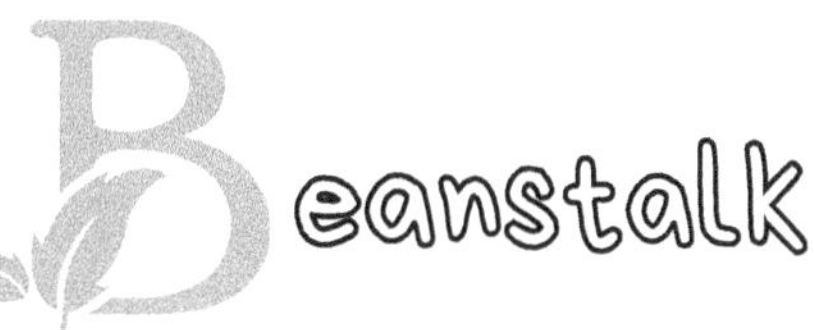eanstalk 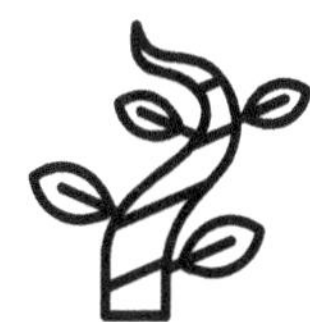

**Challenge:**
Take a photo of your child hugging the widest tree (beanstalk)
in the playground/park.

Date:                  Location:

Today's
weather 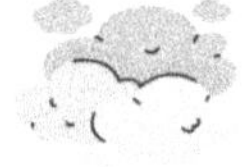 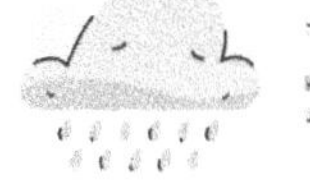 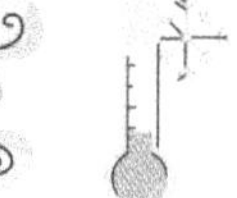

How many
people?

If you were given magic beans, where would you plant them?

Would you rather be a giant or have a golden goose?

What would you do if you found yourself small in a giant world?

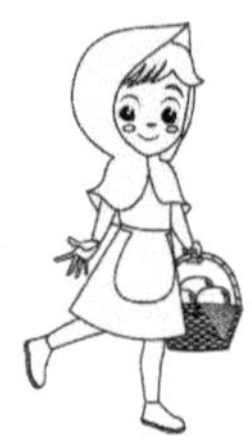 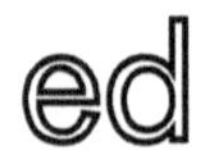 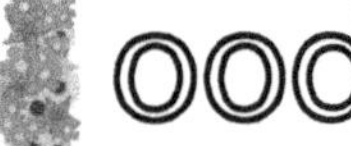

# Little Red Riding Hood

**Challenge:**
Take a picture of your child sticking out from behind a tree
at the park/playground.

Date: Location:

Today's weather 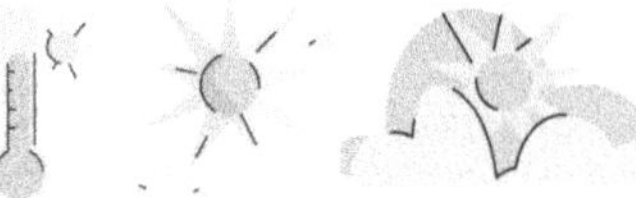 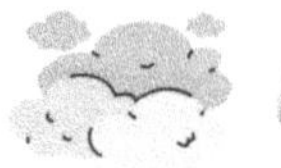 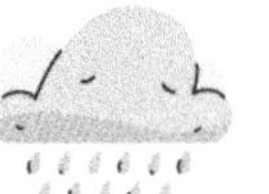 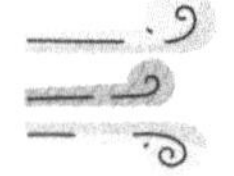 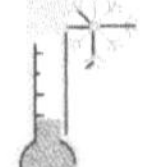

How many people? 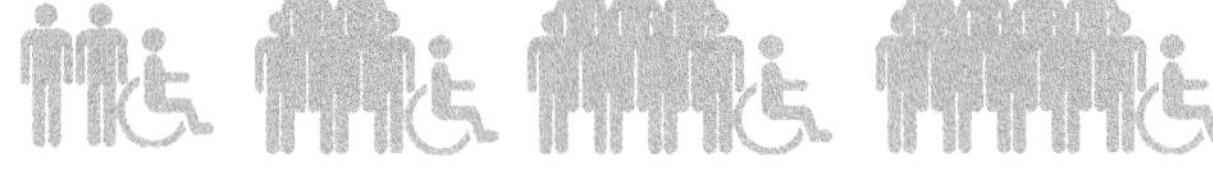

Would you rather be Little Red Riding Hood or the Big Bad Wolf?

What is your favourite flower to pick and give to your parents?

Who would you call if you found a wolf dressed as your grandparent?

# 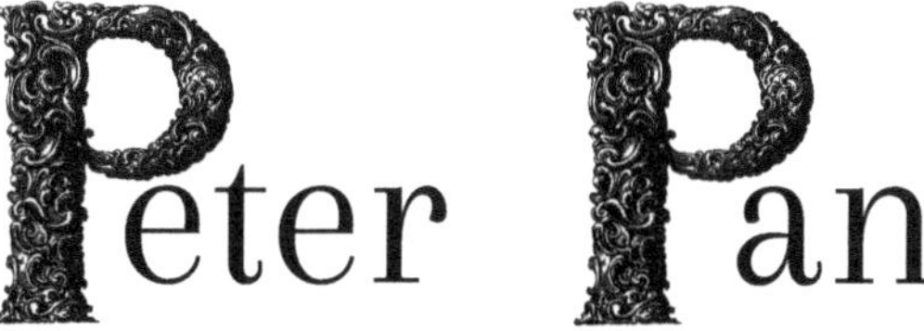Peter Pan 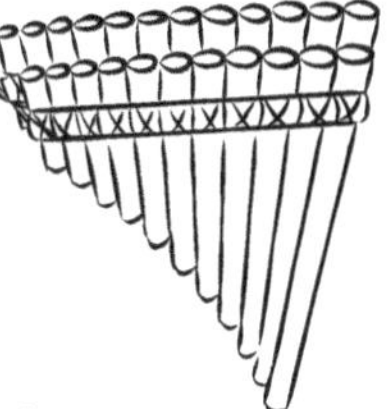

**Challenge:**
Take a photo of your child pretending to fly like Peter Pan or Wendy
at the playground/park.

Date:                               Location:

Today's
 weather          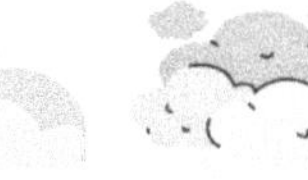 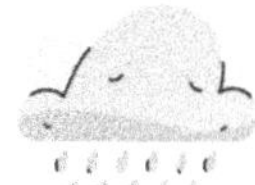 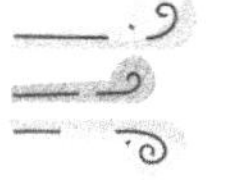 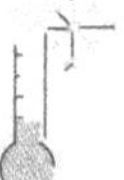

How many
people?          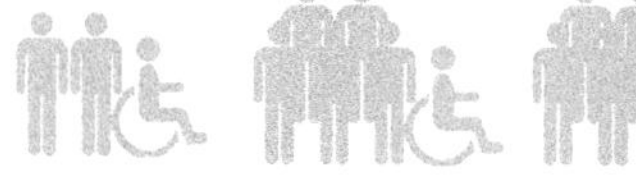 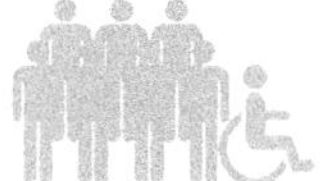 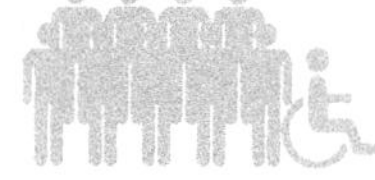

If you could stay a child forever, what would you do?


What colour would your outfit be if you were a fairy like Tinkerbell?


Where would you go, if you could fly anywhere in the world?

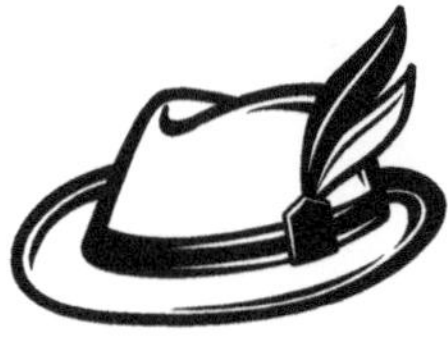

# Pinocchio

**Challenge:**
Take a photo of your child with a stick as a nose.

Date:                              Location:

Today's
weather      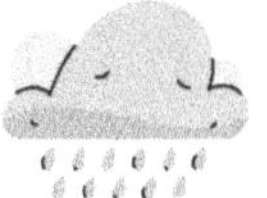 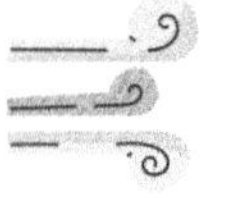 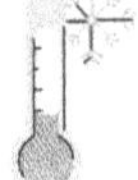

How many
people?     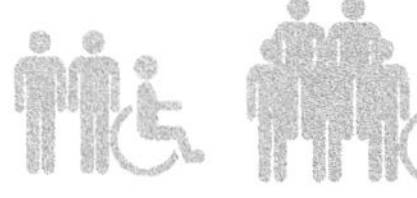 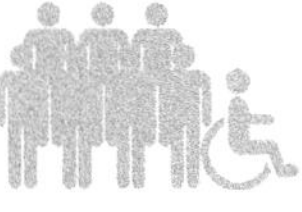 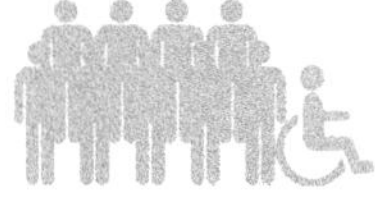

What would you do if your nose grew every time you lied?


If you were turned into a puppet who could talk, what would you do?


Would you rather be swallowed then spat out by a whale or turned into a talking donkey?

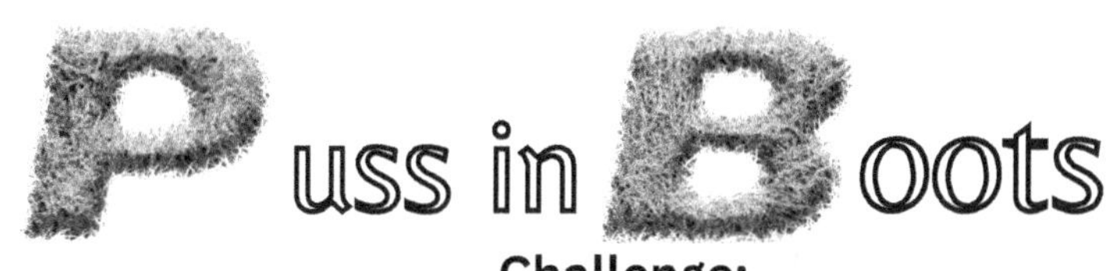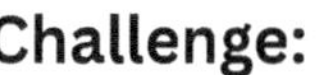

# Puss in Boots

**Challenge:**
Take a photo of your child pretending to have a sword fight.

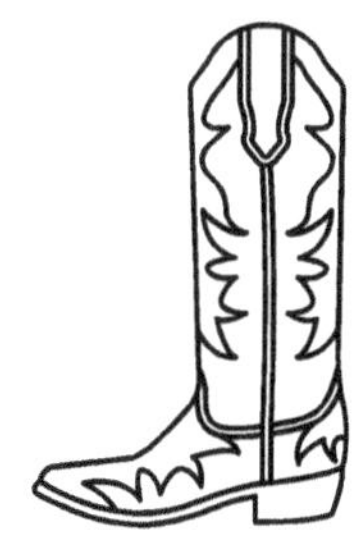

Date:                          Location:

Today's
weather
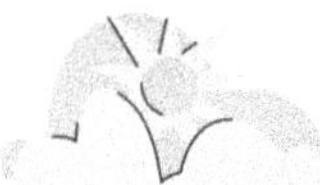 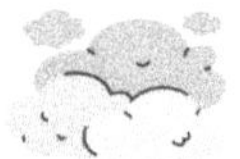 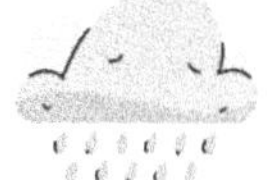 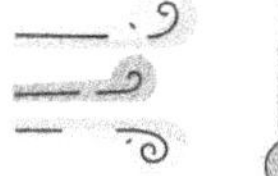 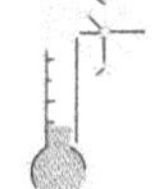

How many
people?

Where would you sleep if you were a cat?


Would you rather be Puss in Boots or a farmer?


Which of your parents do you think would win a sword fight?

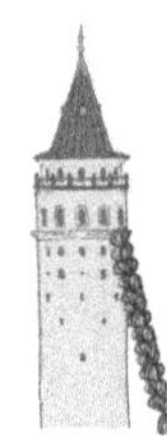

# *Rapunzel*

**Challenge:**
Take a photo of your child on the highest platform they can comfortably and safely get to at the playground.

Date:                    Location:

Today's weather 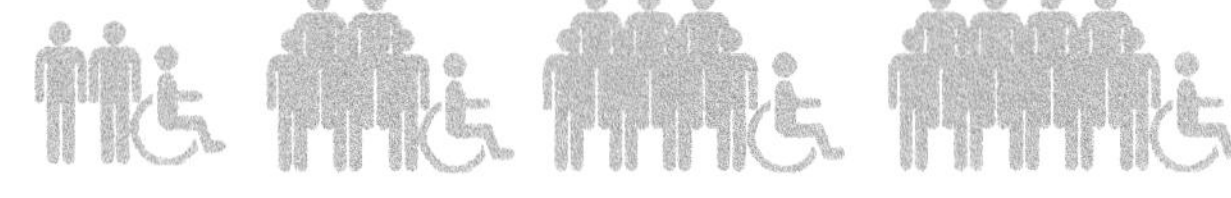

How many people? 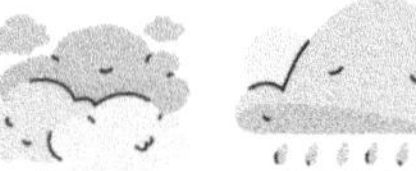 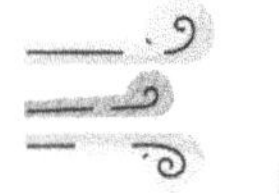 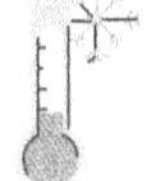

What is your favourite equipment to climb?

Where is your favourite place to brush or style your hair?

If you lived in a tower, what would you do all day?

# Robinhood

**Challenge:**

Take a photo of your child pretending to shoot a bow and arrow.

Date:                          Location:

Today's
weather

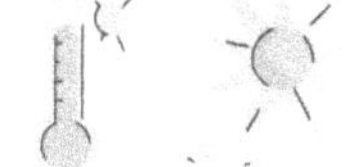 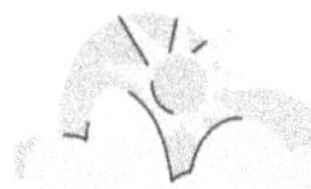 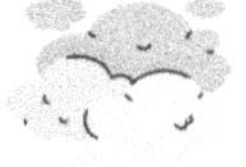 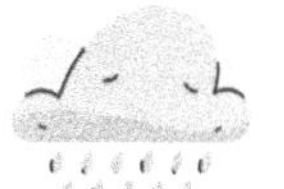 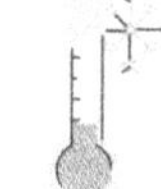

How many
people?

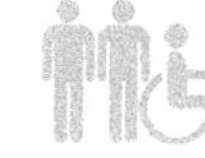 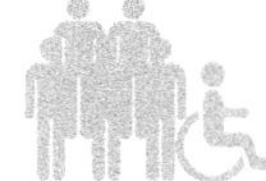 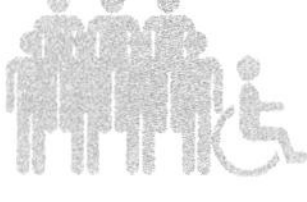 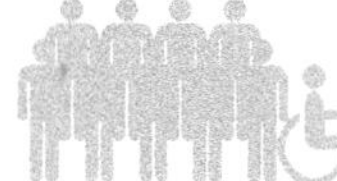

If you were Robinhood would you steal from the rich, to give to the poor?

Would you rather be Little John or Robinhood?

Have you ever shot a bow and arrow? Would do it or do it again?

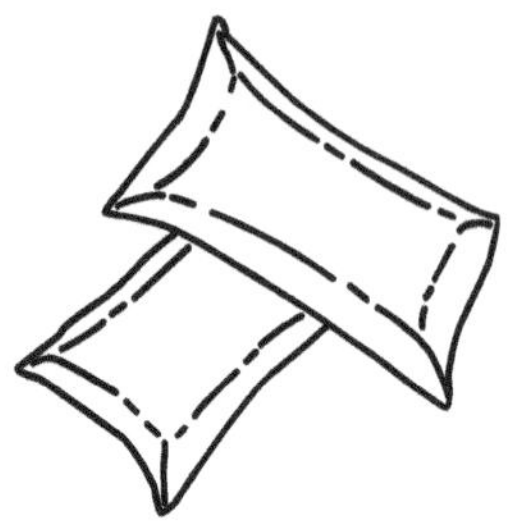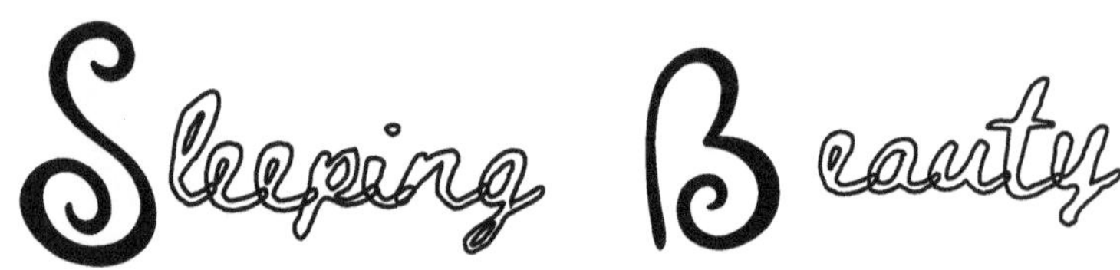



**Challenge:**
Take a photo of your child pretending to be asleep
at the playground.

Date:                          Location:

Today's
weather          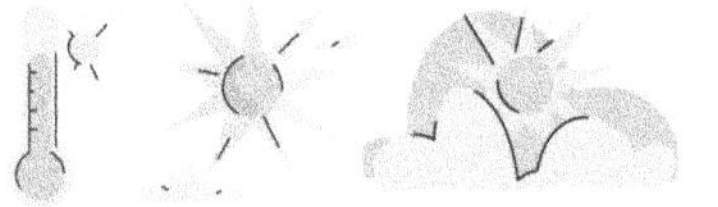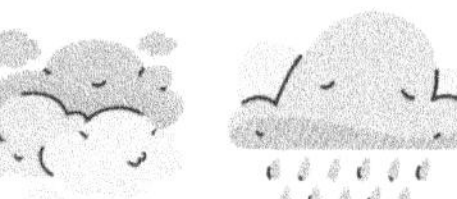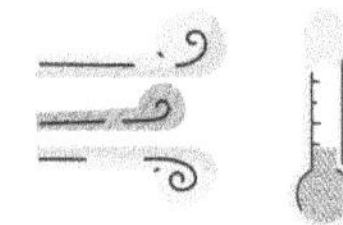

How many
people?          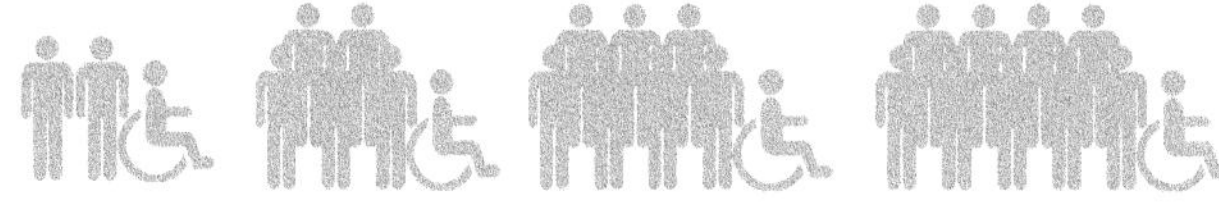

What made you laugh at the playground today?

Where is your favourite place to have a naps?

If you could remember every dream, would you tell others or keep them to
yourself?

# 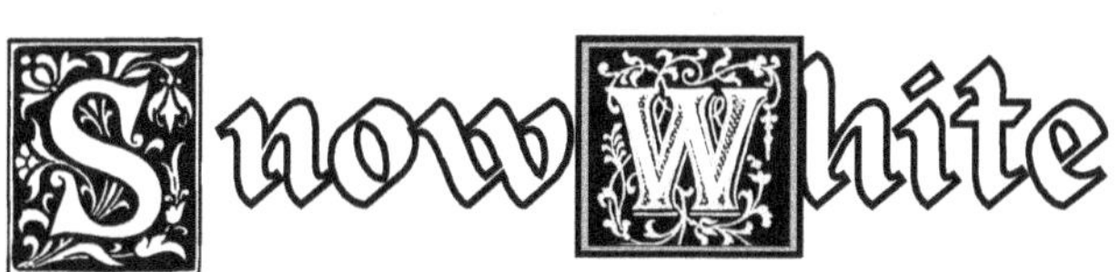Snow White

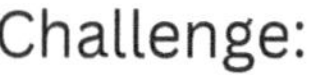
Challenge:
Take a photo of your child pretending to be a dwarf by
kneeling on their shoes and holding an apple.

Date:                      Location:

Today's
weather 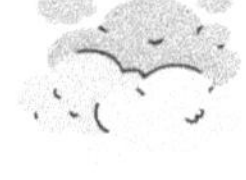 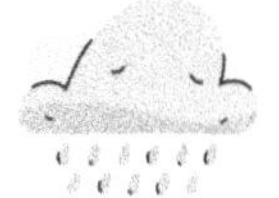 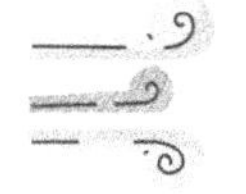 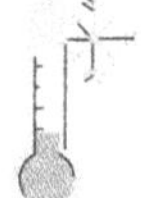

How many
people?

Would you rather clean your bedroom or clean the living room?

Do you prefer to eat red or green apples?

If you were a dwarf, who would you be? (Doc, Grumpy, Happy, Sleepy, Bashful,
Sneeze, or Dopey) Why?

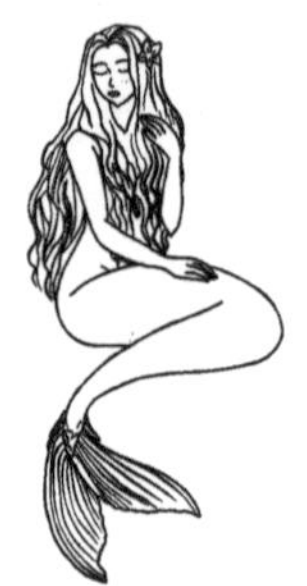

# The Little Mermaid

**Challenge:**
Take a photo of your child sitting on/near a rock
and pretending to brush their hair.

Date:                              Location:

Today's weather 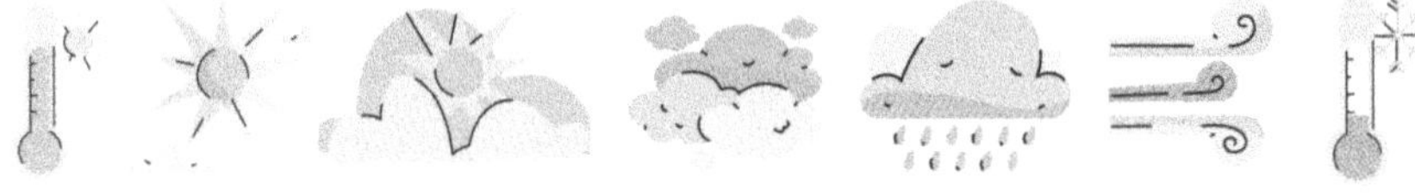

How many people? 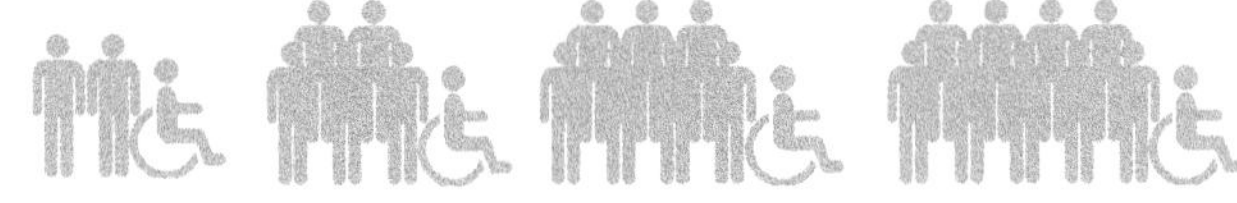

Would you rather sing with a crab or swim with a dolphin?

Where is your favourite place at home to brush your hair?

If you were a mermaid/merman, what colour would your tail be?

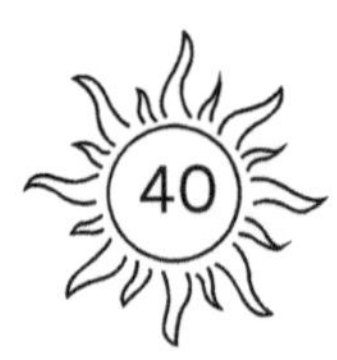

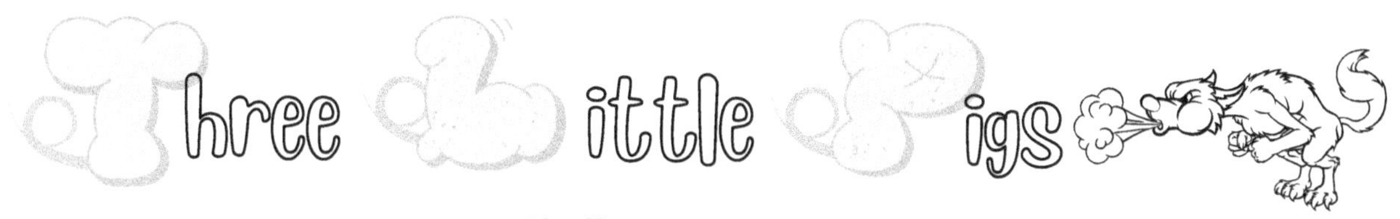


**Challenge:**
Take a photo of your child and a house of sticks that your child made.

Date:                        Location:

Today's
weather

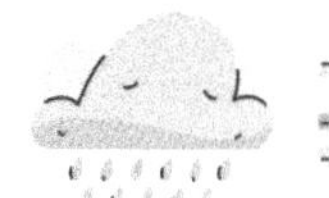
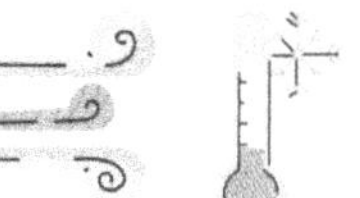

How many
people?

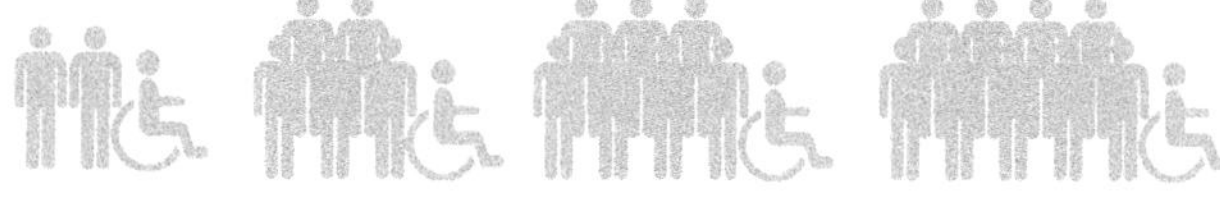

What makes you happy about this playground?

Where would you hide in a playground from the big bad wolf?

If you were a little pig, what would you build your house with?

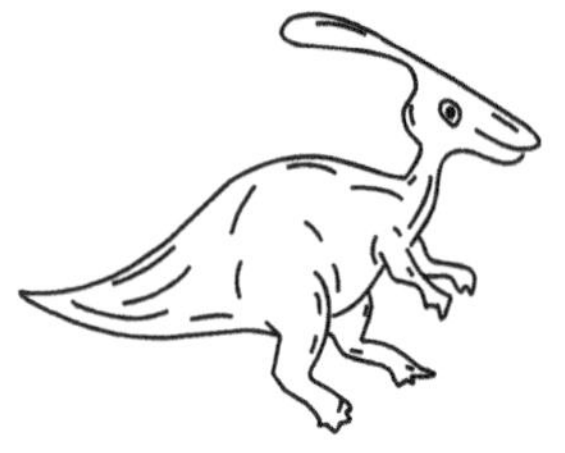
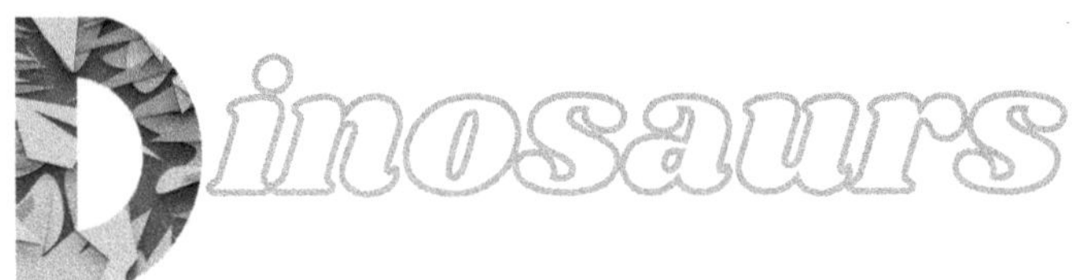

# Dinosaurs

**Challenge:**
Take a photo of your child with
a dinosaur statue that ate grass.

Date:                              Location:

Today's
weather
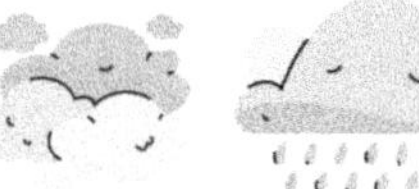  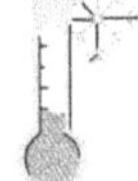

How many
people?
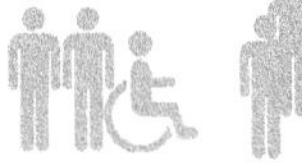 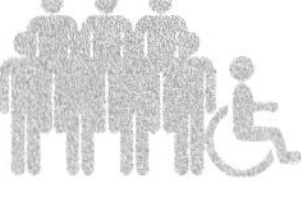 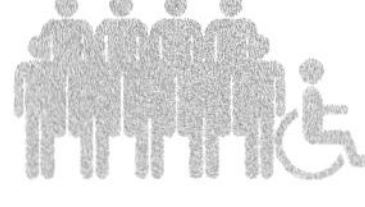

What type of dinosaur did you take a picture with?

If you could be any dinosaur, what would you be?

Where would you live if you were a dinosaur?

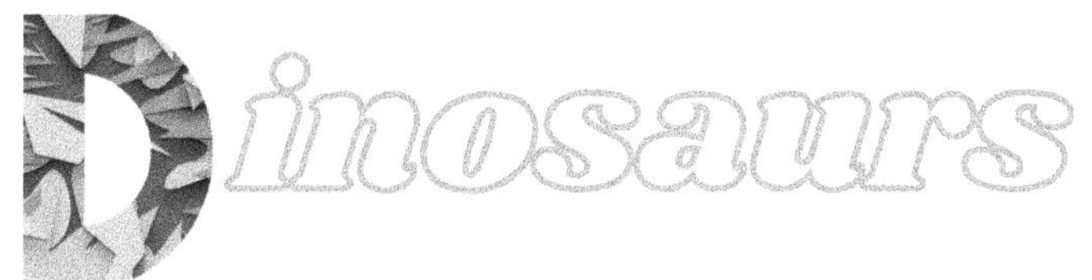 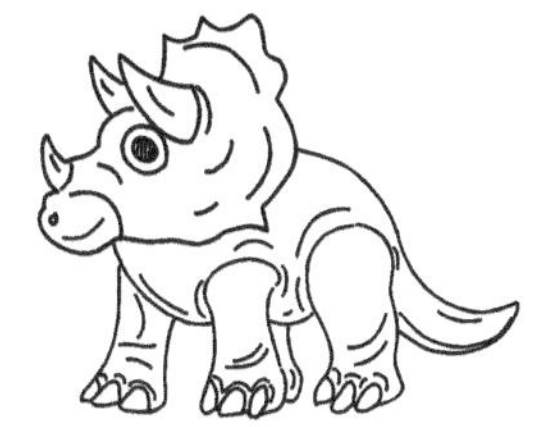

# Dinosaurs

**Challenge:**
Take a photo of your child with
a dinosaur statue that has horns.

Date:                    Location:

Today's
 weather
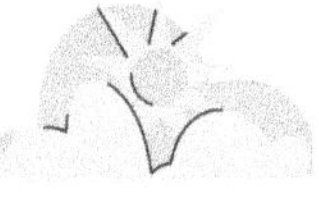 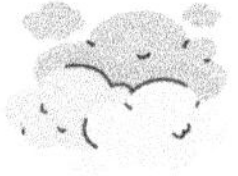 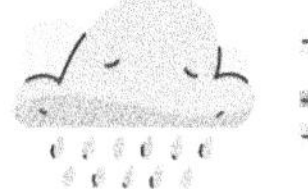 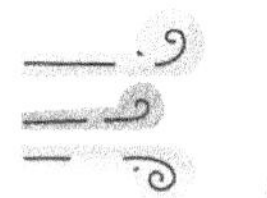 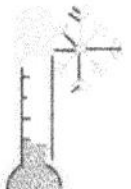

How many
people?
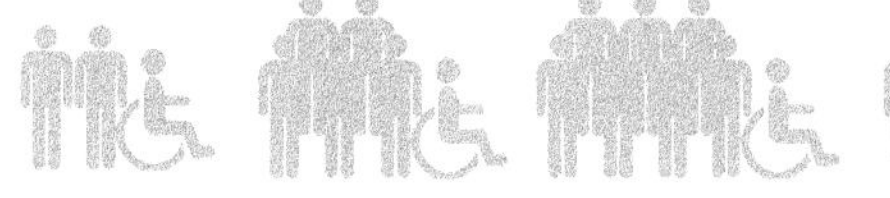

What type of dinosaur did you take a picture with?

Is this a meat eating or a vegetation eating type of dinosaur?

Do you think this dinosaur lived in a forest or in a desert?

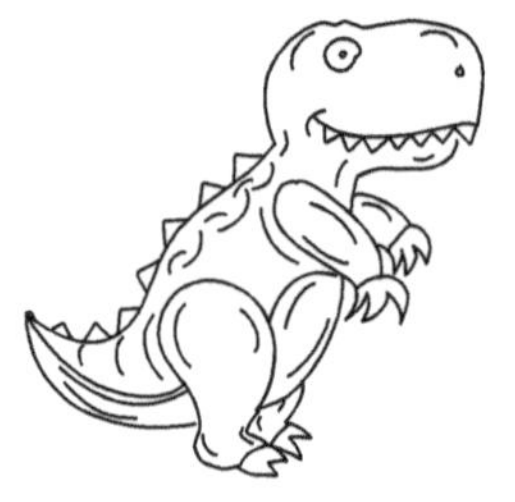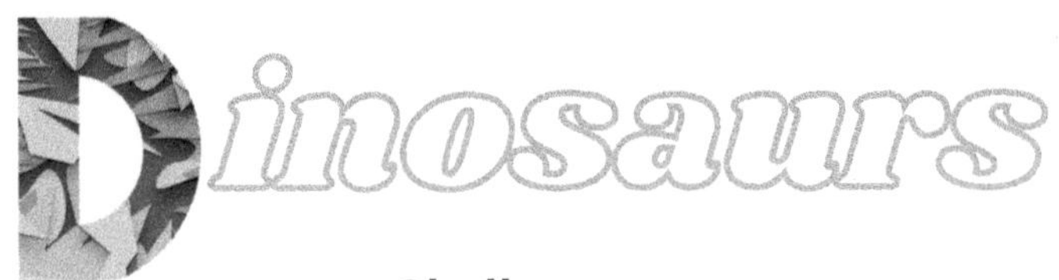

# Dinosaurs

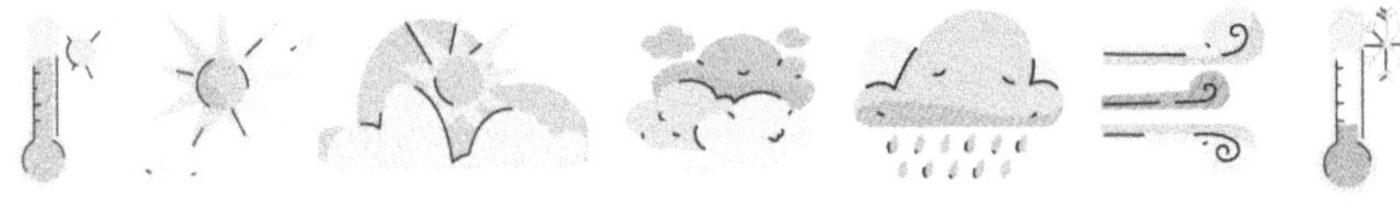
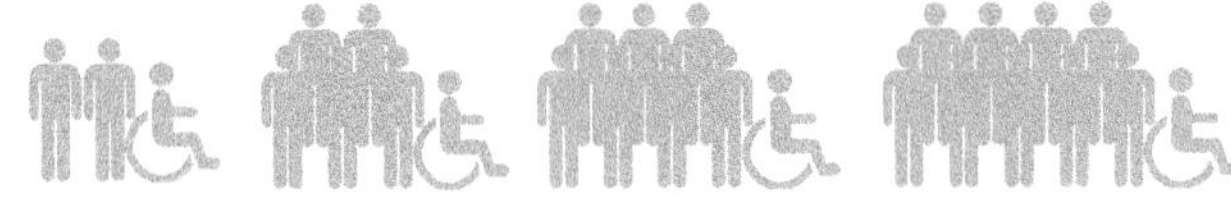

**Challenge:**
Take a photo of your child with
a dinosaur statue that has sharp teeth.

Date:                    Location:

Today's
weather

How many
people?

What type of dinosaur did you take a picture with?


Do you think this dinosaur could run really fast or only walk slowly?


If you were this dinosaur, where would you live?

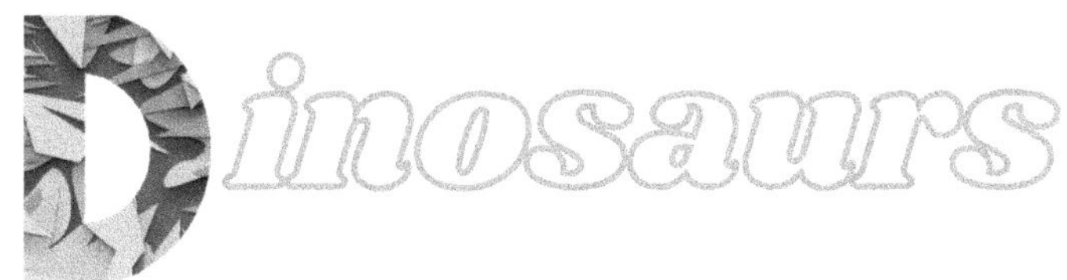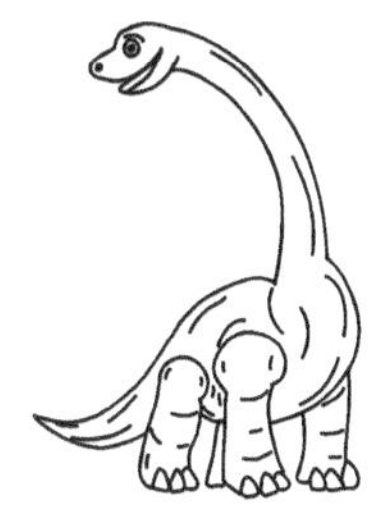

**Challenge:**
Take a photo of your child with
a dinosaur statue that has a long neck.

Date:                    Location:

Today's
weather 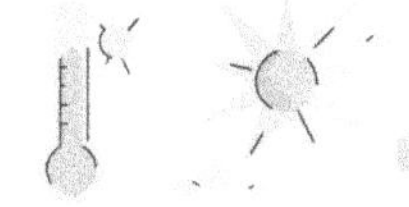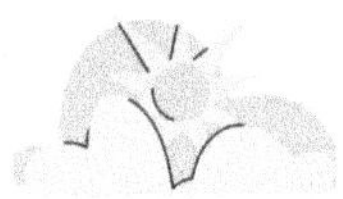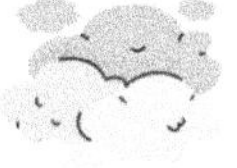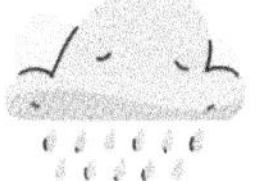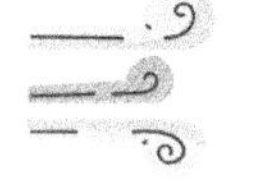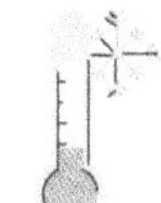

How many
people? 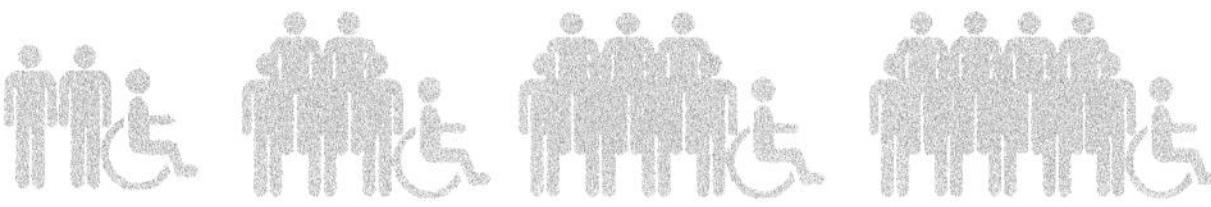

What type of dinosaur did you take a picture with?

Do you think this dinosaur has sharp teeth or blunt teeth?

If you could ride any dinosaur, which one would you choose?

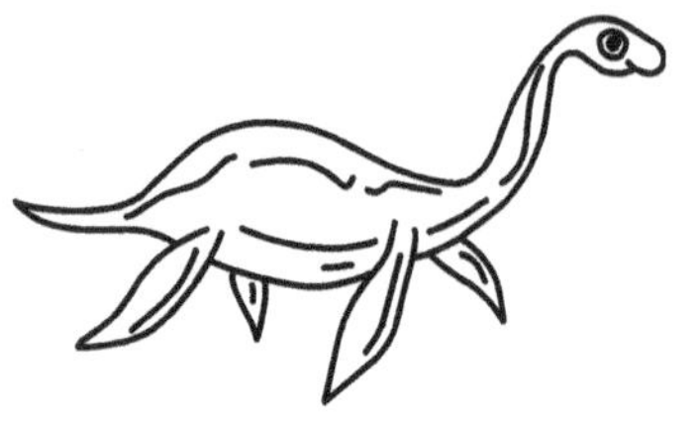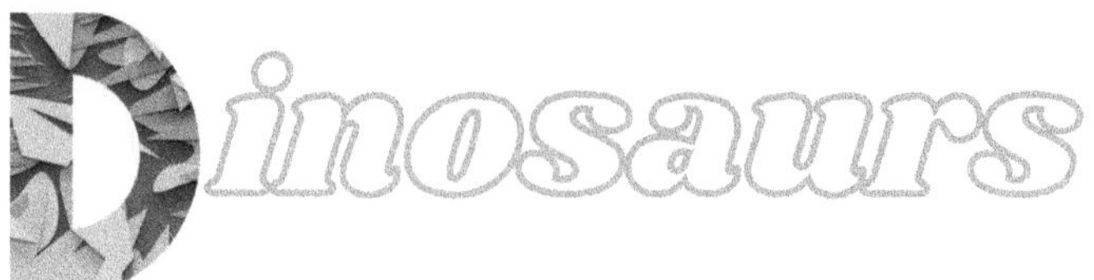

**Challenge:**
Take a photo of your child with
a dinosaur statue that could swim.

Date:                              Location:

Today's
weather
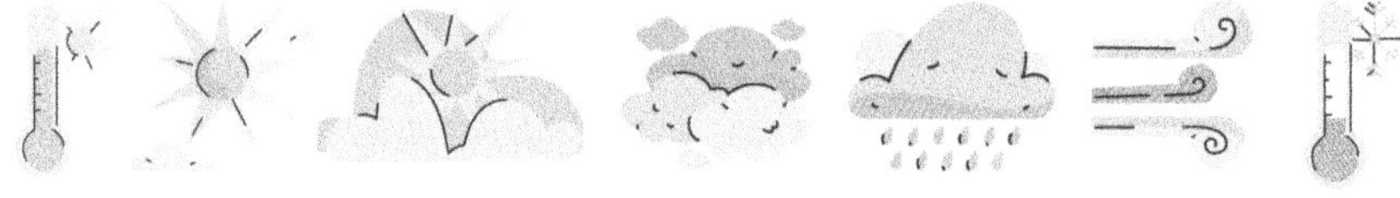

How many
people?
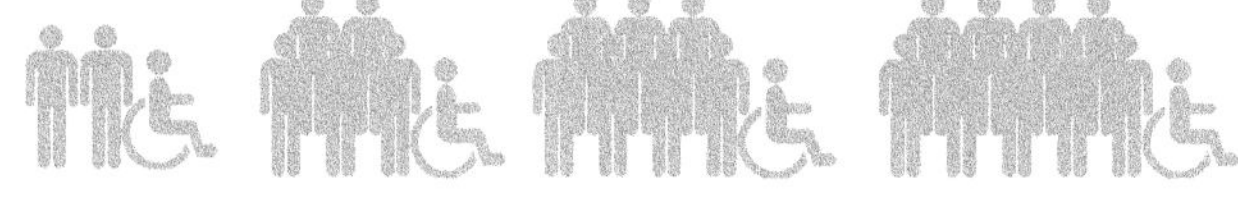

What type of dinosaur did you take a picture with?


Does your dinosaur live on land or in the water?


Would you have this type of dinosaur as a pet? Why/why not?

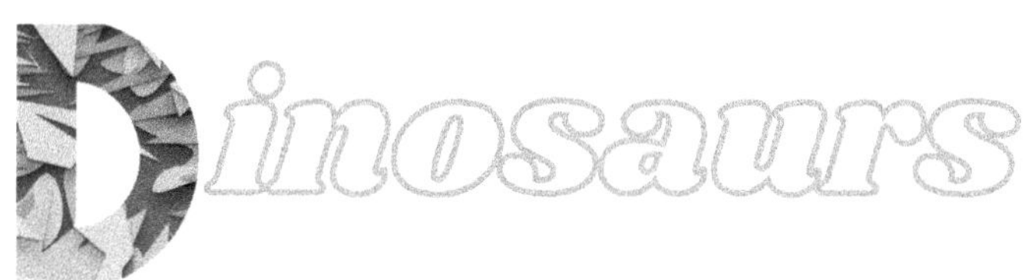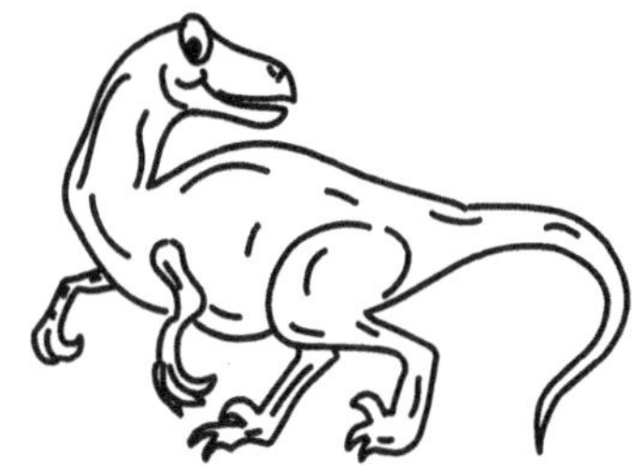

# Dinosaurs

**Challenge:**
Take a photo of your child with
a dinosaur statue that has sharp claws.

Date:                              Location:

Today's
 weather
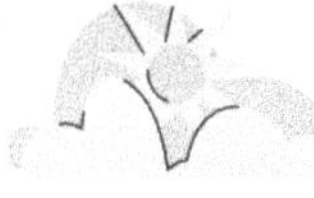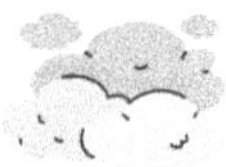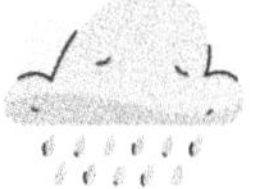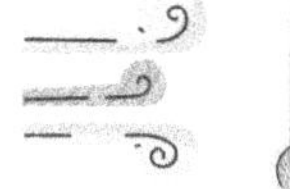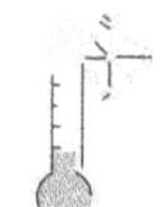

How many
people?
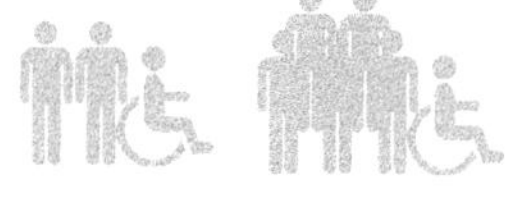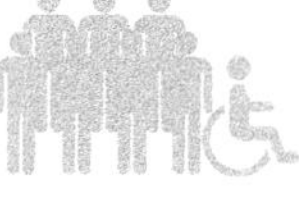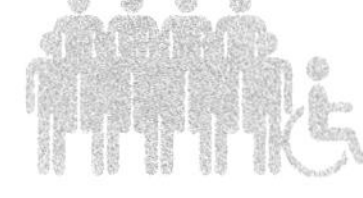

What type of dinosaur did you take a picture with?


Does your dinosaur run on two legs or on four legs?


Where does your dinosaur live? Forest, desert, lake or ocean?

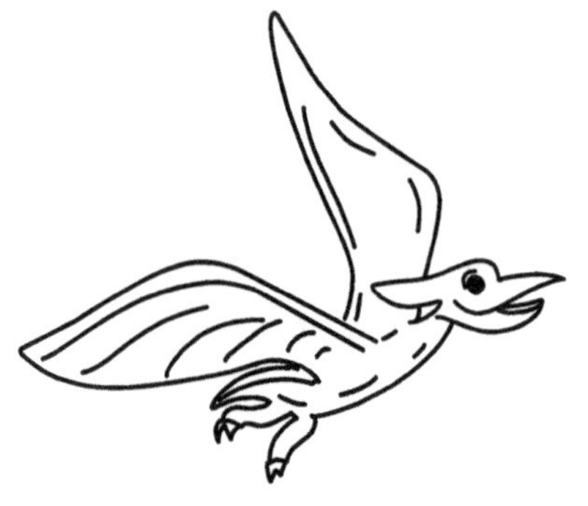 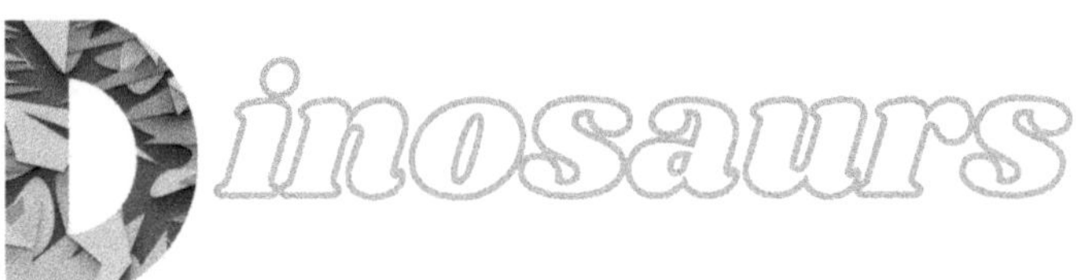

# Dinosaurs

**Challenge:**
Take a photo of your child with
a dinosaur statue that could fly.

Date:                              Location:

Today's
weather

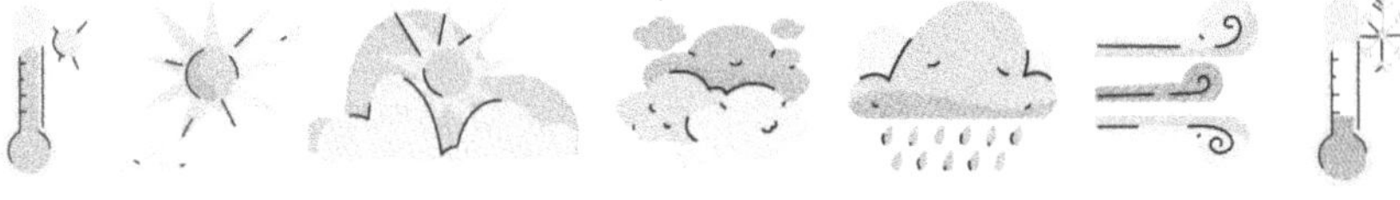

How many
people?

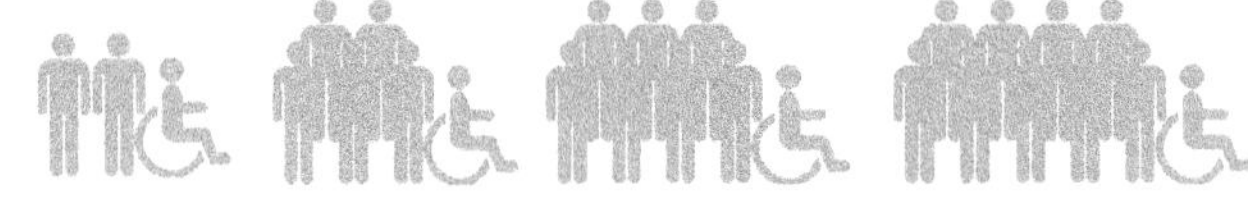

What type of dinosaur did you take a picture with?

Do you think the dinosaur's skin would be rough like sandpaper or smooth like glass?

If you could be a dinosaur that can fly or swim, what would you choose and why?

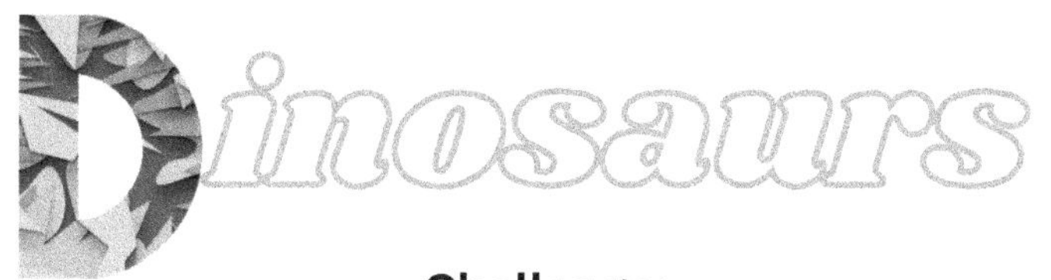 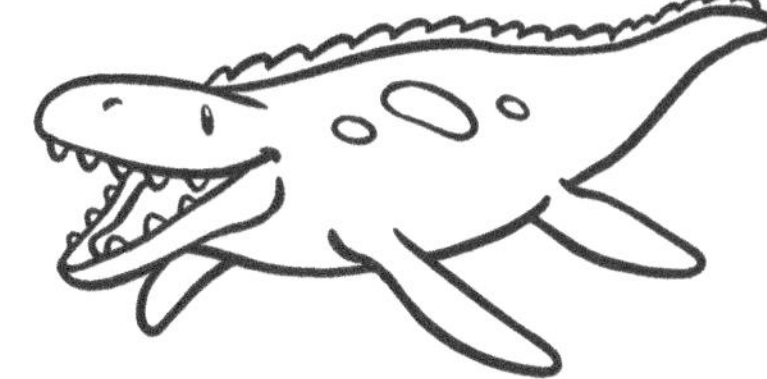

**Challenge:**
Take a photo of your child with
a dinosaur statue that has flippers.

Date:                    Location:

Today's
weather

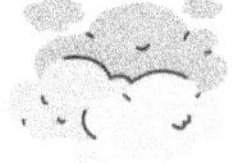 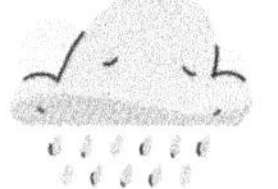 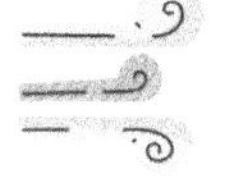 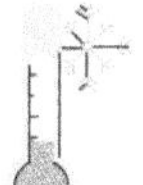

How many
people?

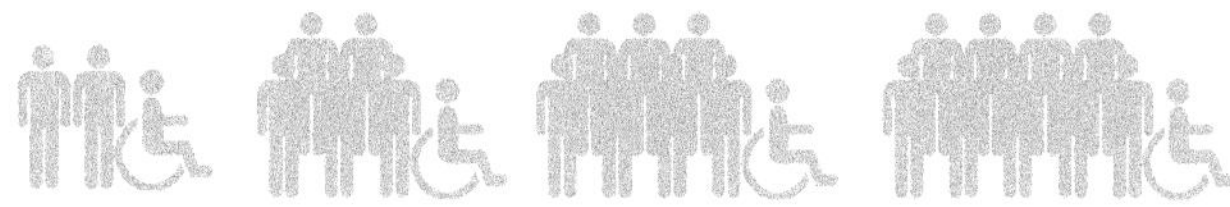

What type of dinosaur did you take a picture with?

If you could live in a lake or an ocean, where would you live?

Which colour would you want your dinosaur to be in real life?

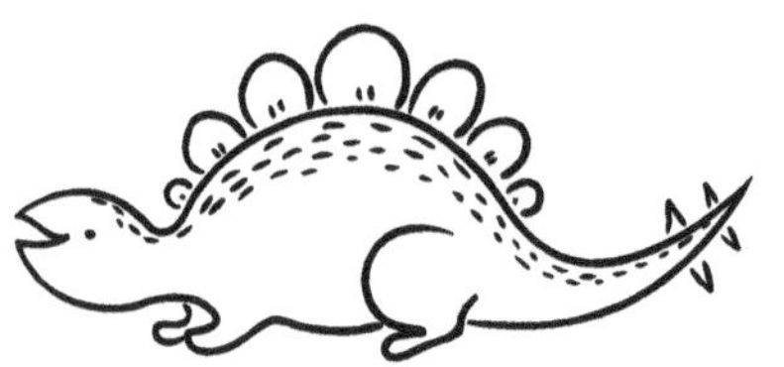 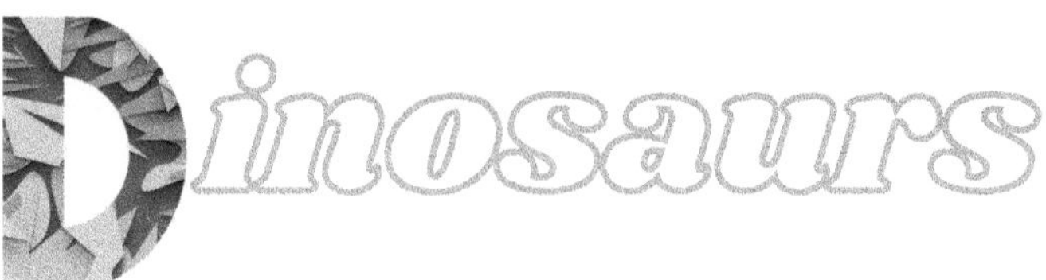

# Dinosaurs

**Challenge:**
Take a photo of your child with
a dinosaur statue that has spikes.

Date:                    Location:

Today's
weather
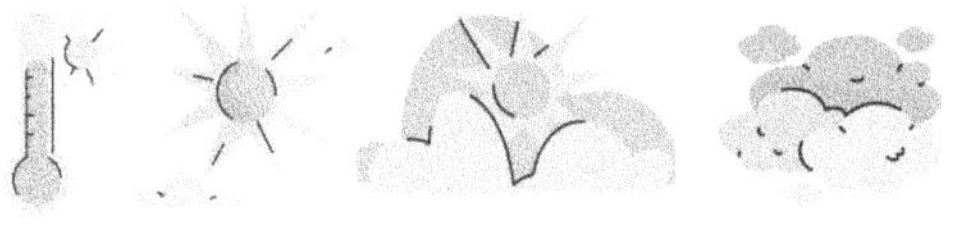 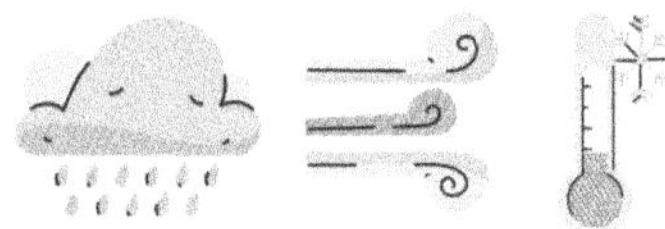

How many
people?
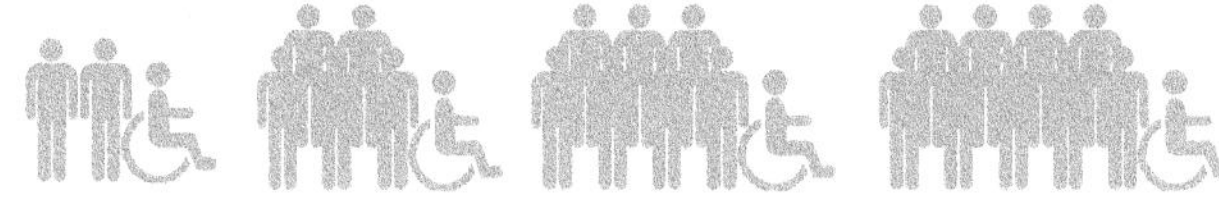

What type of dinosaur did you take a picture with?

Do you think you could beat the dinosaur in a running race?

Who would be taller, you or the dinosaur in real life? Are your
parents taller?

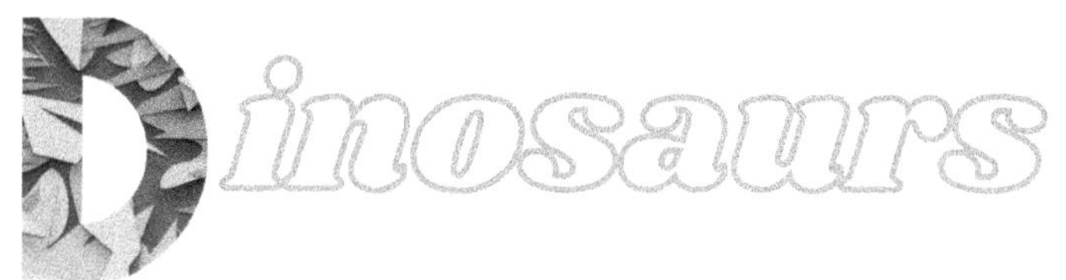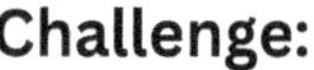
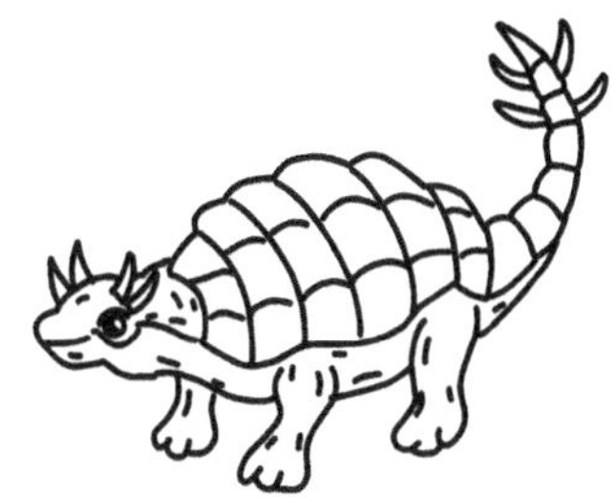

**Challenge:**
Take a photo of your child with
a dinosaur statue that has a long tail.

Date:                                Location:

Today's
weather 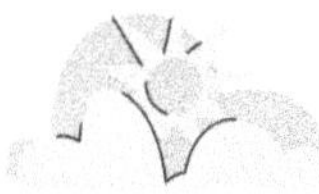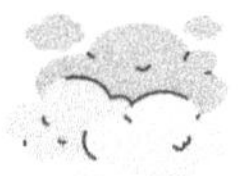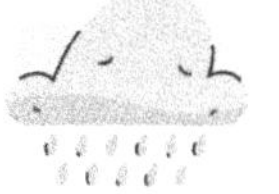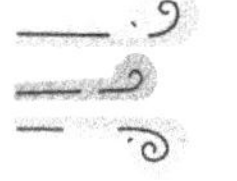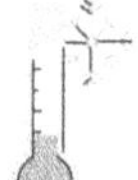

How many
people? 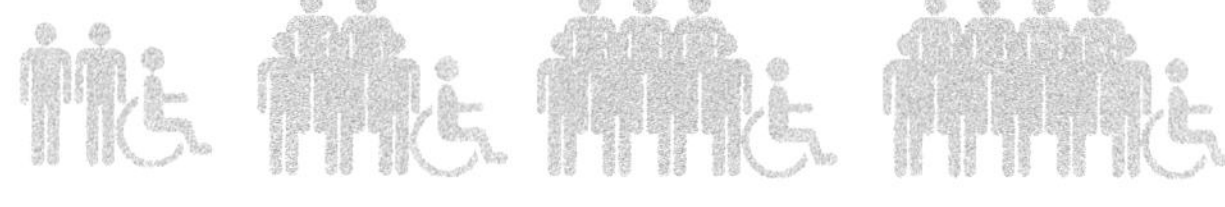

What type of dinosaur did you take a picture with?

Who do you think would have bigger teeth? What about bigger toe nails?

If you could take a dinosaur for a walk, where would you go with it?

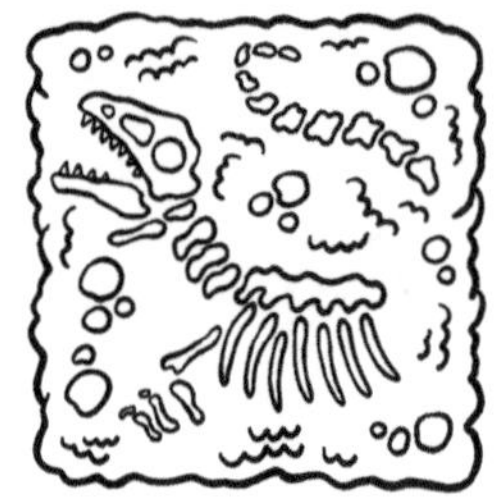
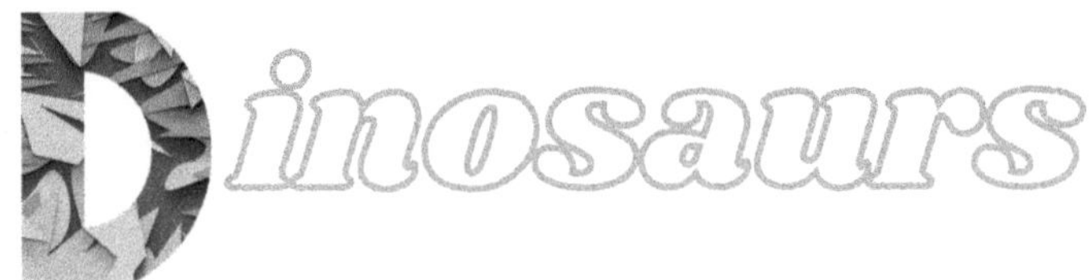

Challenge:
Take a photo of your child with
a dinosaur fossil statue.

Date:                    Location:

Today's
weather
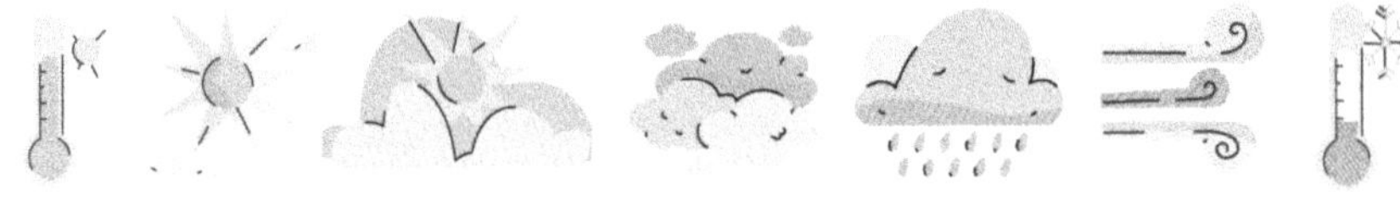

How many
people?
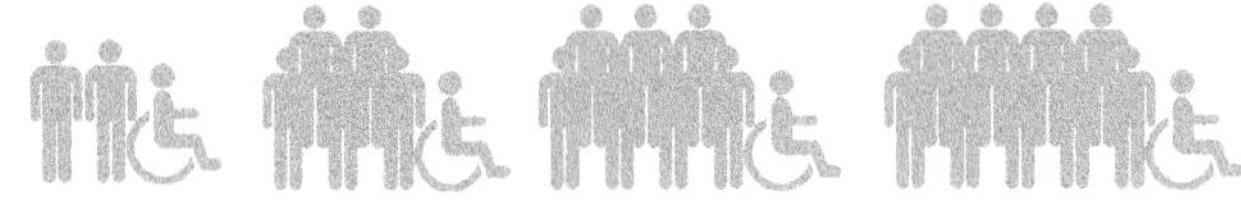

What type of dinosaur made this fossil?




If you were digging out a fossil, what type of tools would you use?




Where would you put a fossil in your house, if you found one?

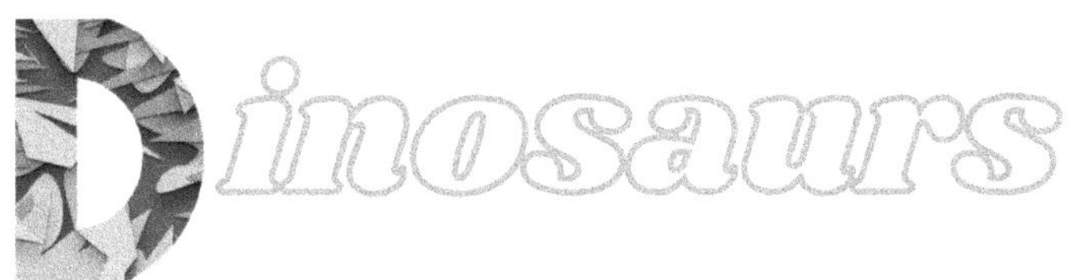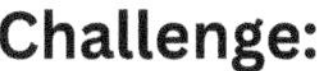# Dinosaurs

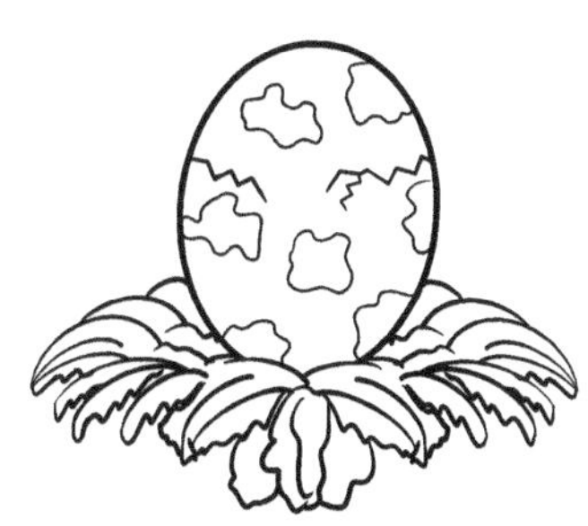

**Challenge:**
Take a photo of your child with
a dinosaur nest and egg statue.

Date:                    Location:

Today's
weather 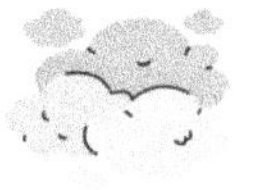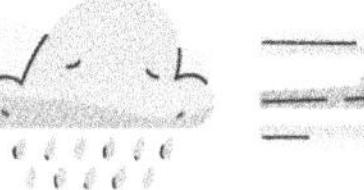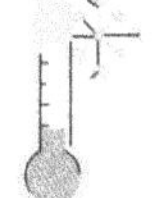

How many
people? 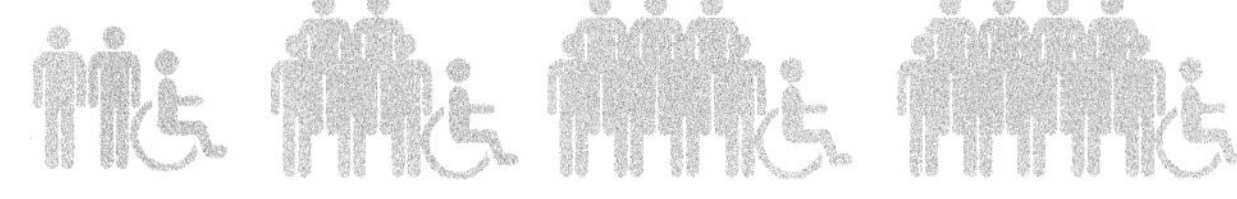

If you were building a nest, where would you put it?

What would you build your nest out of? Why?

Would you rather have one large egg, or a three smaller eggs?

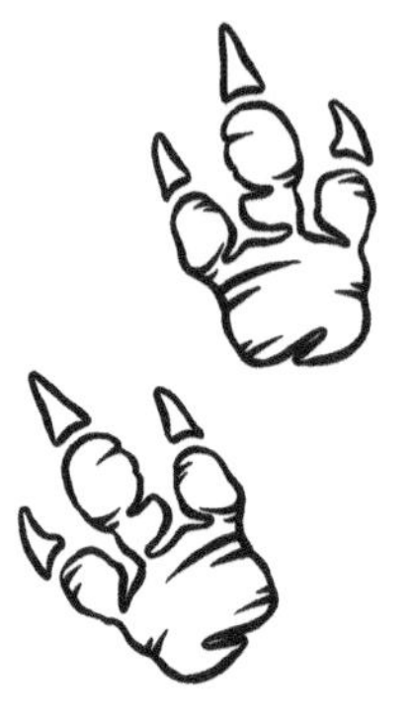 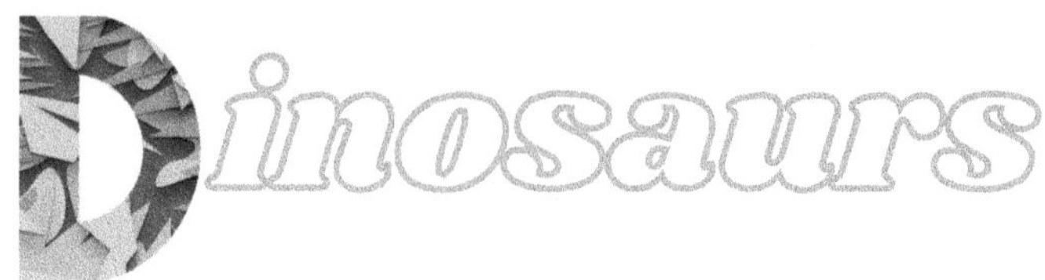

# Dinosaurs

**Challenge:**
Take a photo of your child
with a dinosaur footprint.

Date:                    Location:

Today's
weather
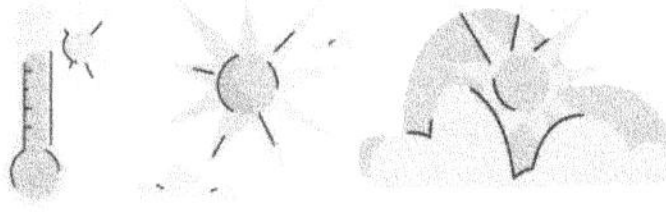 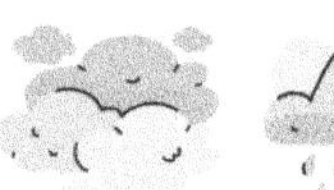 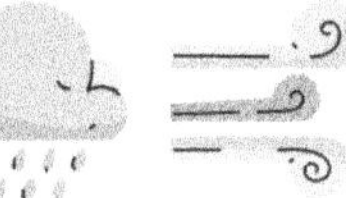 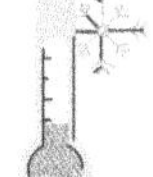

How many
people?
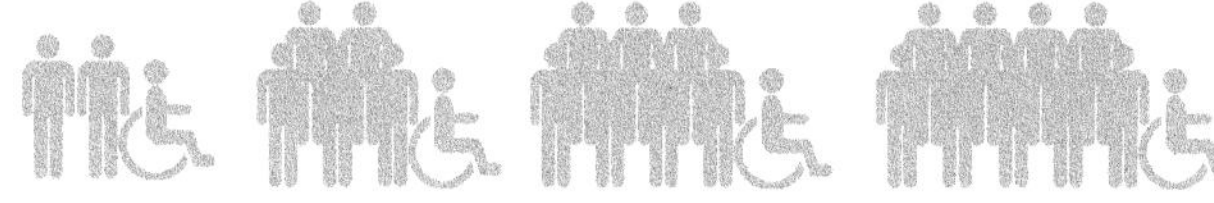

Who has the biggest feet? You, your parent, or the dinosaur?

If you could make a footprint that would last forever, where would you leave it?

Would a heavy dinosaur or a light dinosaur make a deeper footprint in mud? Why?

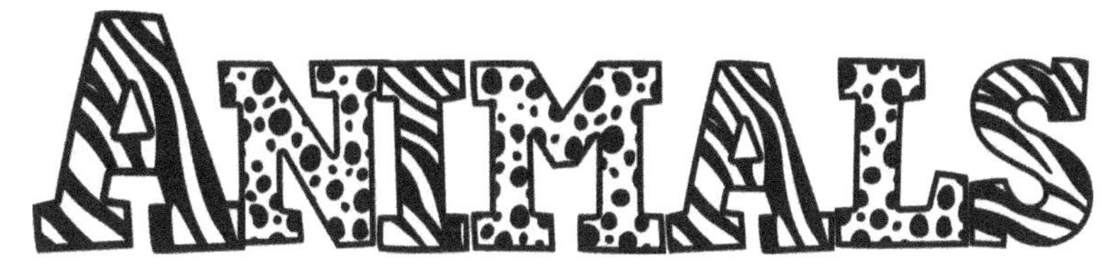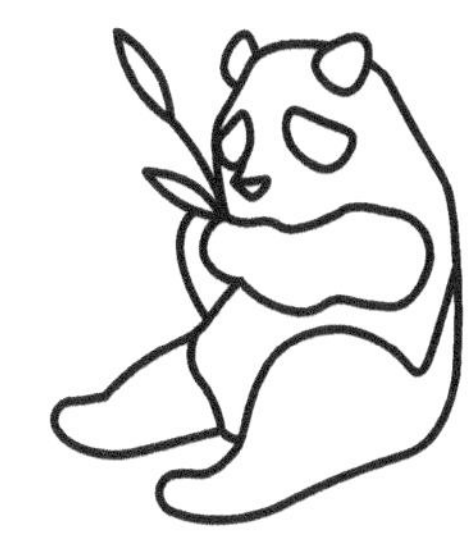

# ANIMALS

**Challenge:**
Take a photo of your child with
a statue of an animal that eats plants.

Date:                    Location:

Today's
 weather
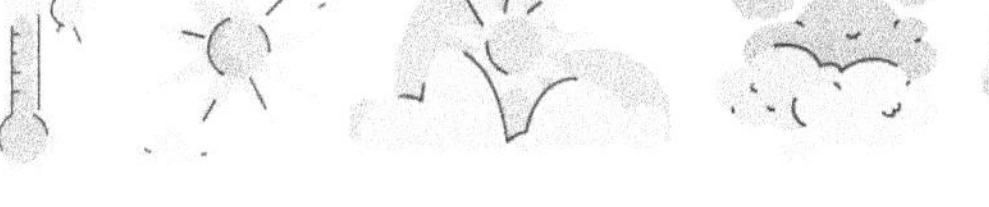

How many
people?
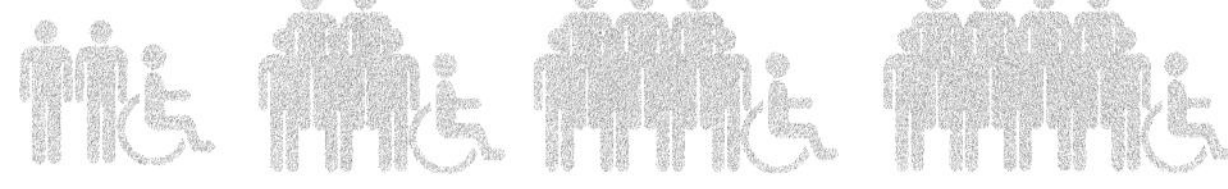

Would you rather eat only bamboo or grass for your whole life?


Where would you prefer to live if you were a panda, in the zoo or in the
bamboo forest?


If you could re-colour a panda, what colours would you pick?:

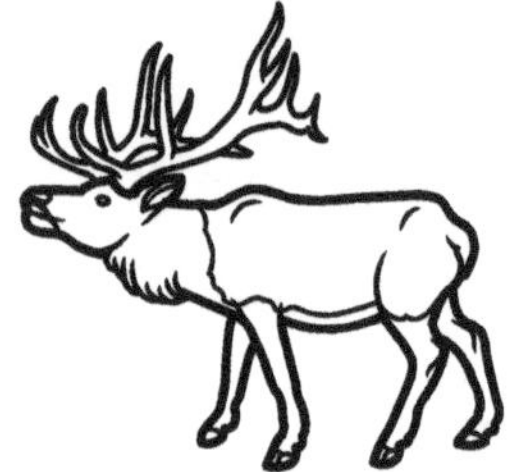 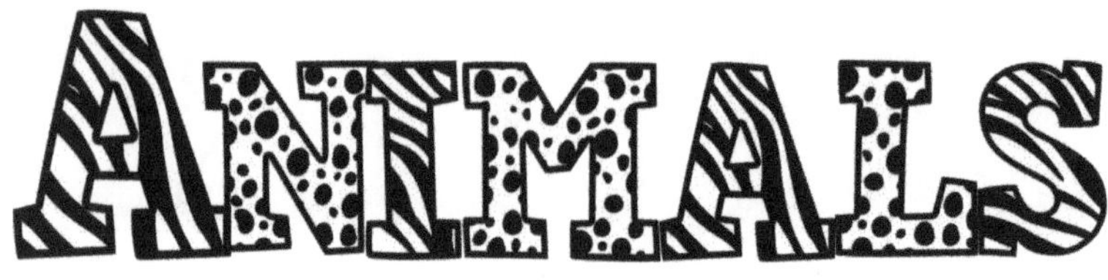

**Challenge:**
Take a photo of your child with
a statue of an animal that has antlers/horns.

Date:                              Location:

Today's
weather
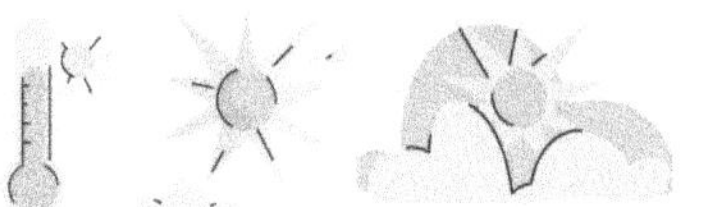 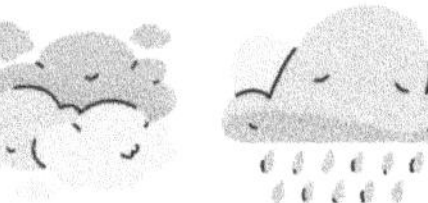 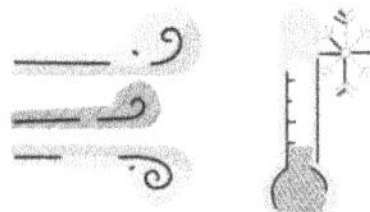

How many
people?
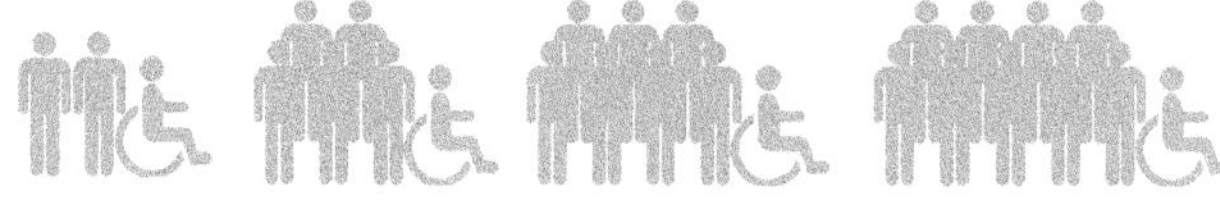

What play equipment do you think a moose would like to use?


Would you rather have large antlers or sharp horns?


If you could choose to be a moose or a ram, which would you pick?

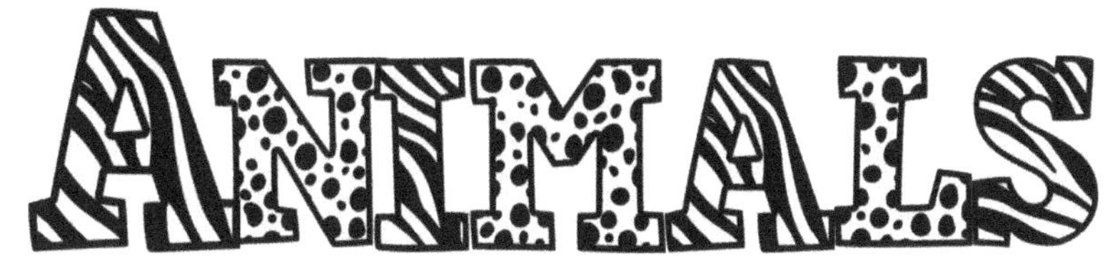

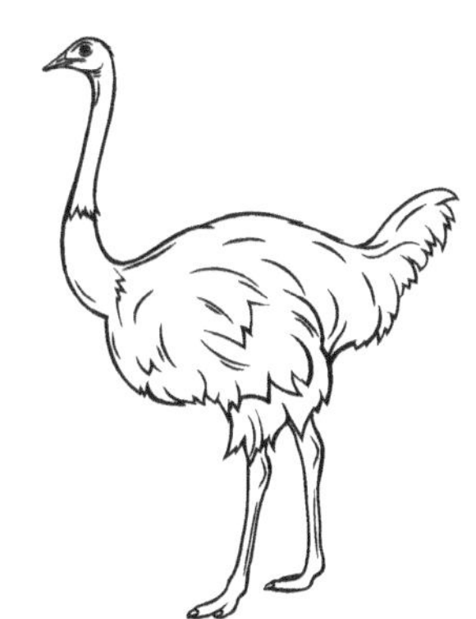

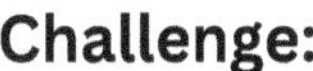

**Challenge:**
Take a photo of your child with
a statue of an animal that has feathers.

Date:                    Location:

Today's
weather

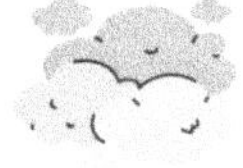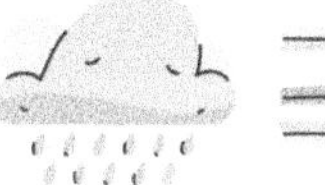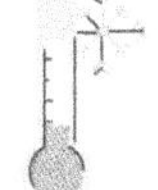

How many
people?

If you could choose to be a really fast bird that runs, or a fast flying bird,
which would you choose?

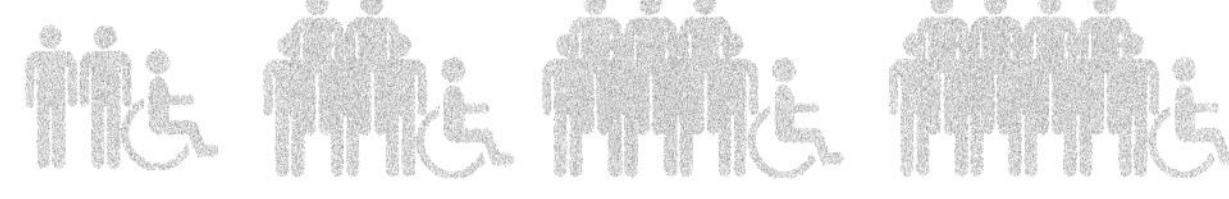

What colours would your feathers be, if you were a bird?

Would you rather have a beautiful voice or be able to see over large
distances?

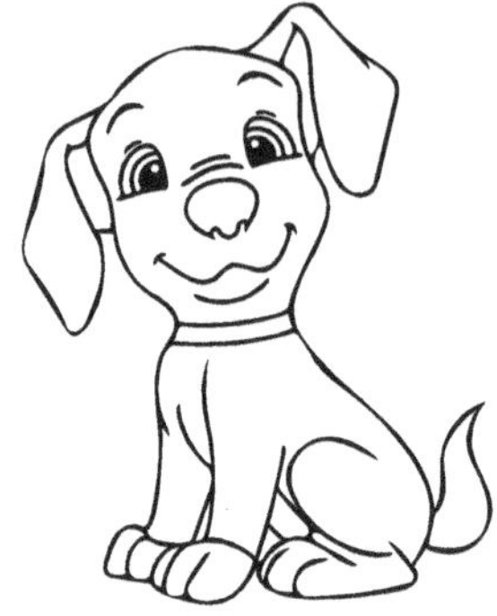

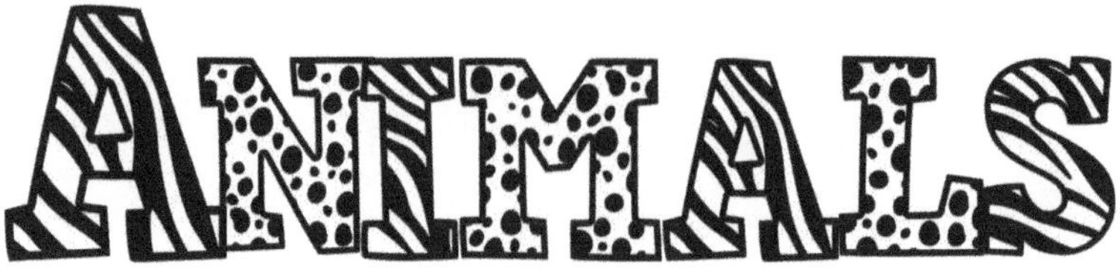



**Challenge:**
Take a photo of your child with
a statue of an animal that can be a pet.

Date:                          Location:

Today's
weather

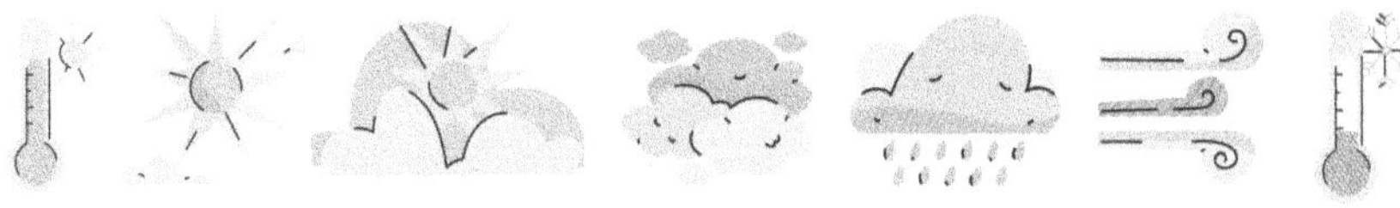

How many
people?

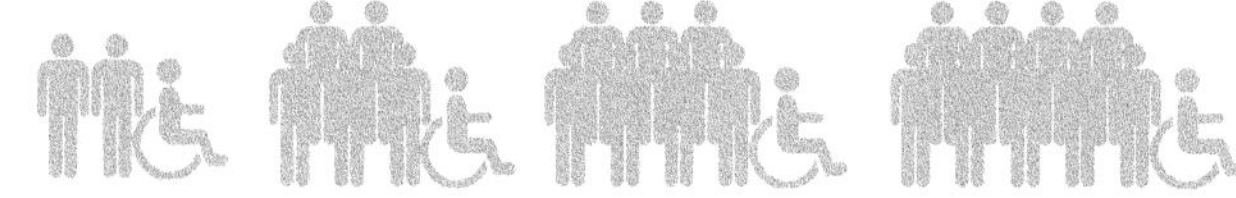

If you could choose any animal to have as a pet, what would you pick?


Would you rather be a dog or a cat? Why?


Where would you sleep in your house, if you were a pet? Why?

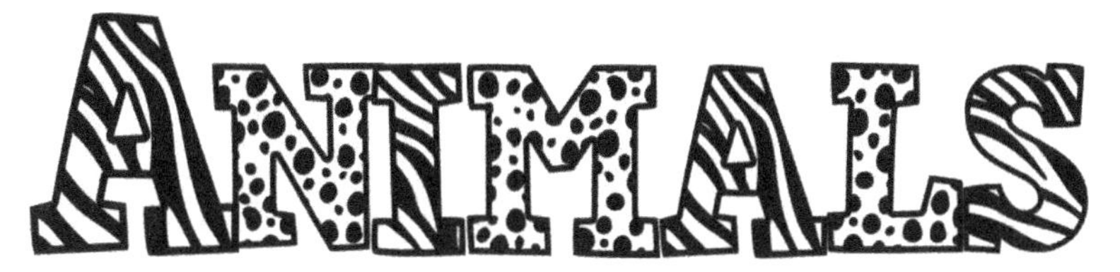


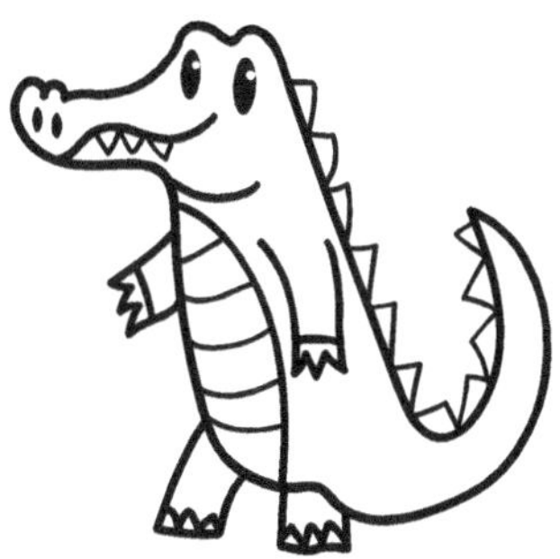

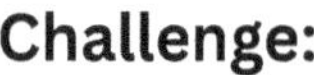
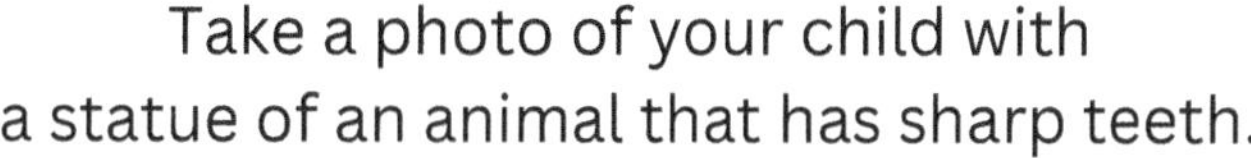

**Challenge:**
Take a photo of your child with
a statue of an animal that has sharp teeth.

Date:                              Location:

Today's
 weather
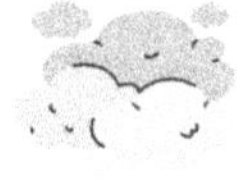 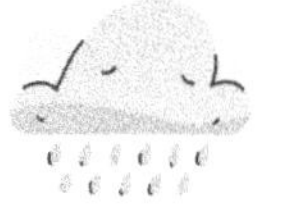 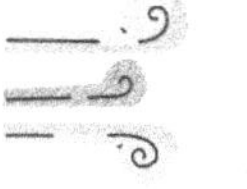 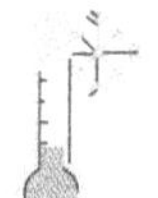

How many
people?

Would you rather be a crocodile or an alligator? Why?

If you had sharp teeth, what would you try to bite?

What game do you think your animal would be good at playing?

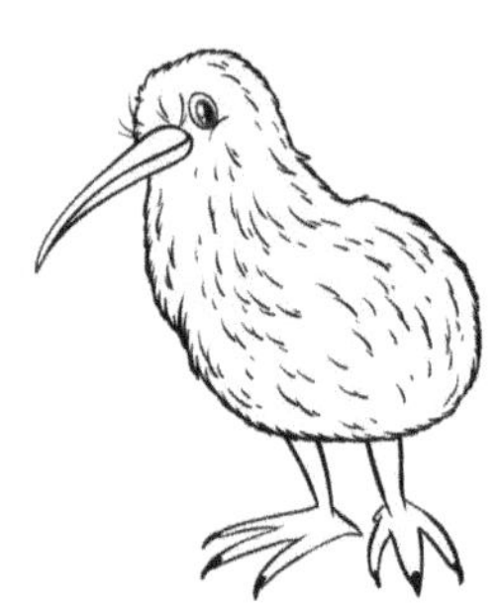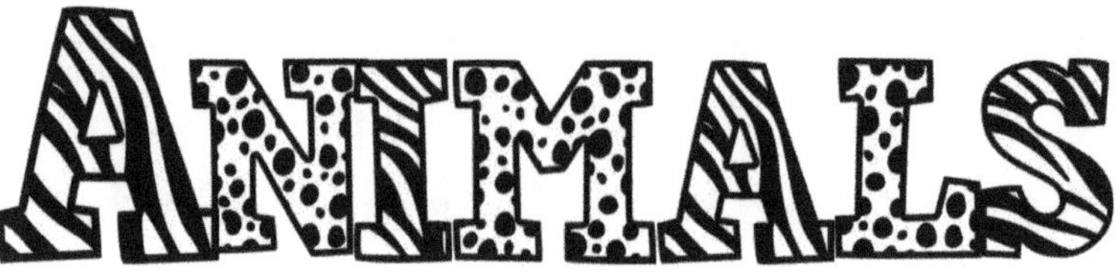

**Challenge:**
Take a photo of your child with
a statue of an animal that comes out at night.

Date:                  Location:

Today's
weather 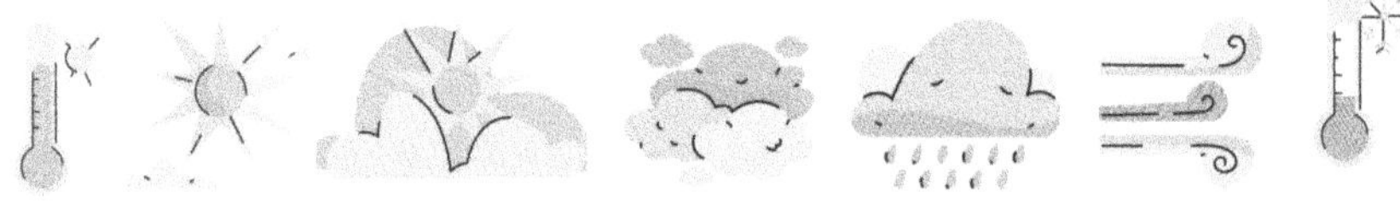

How many
people? 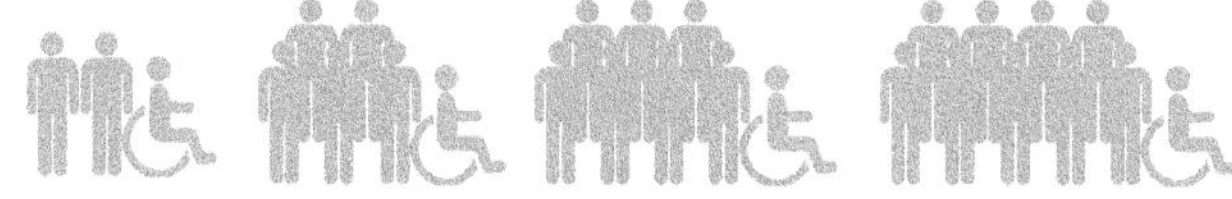

If you woke up at night, what would you do?




Where would you live during the day, if you only came out at night?




What nocturnal animal would you be if you could decide?

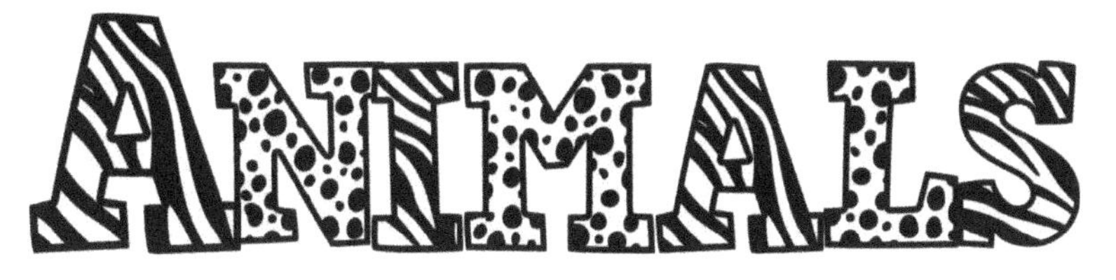

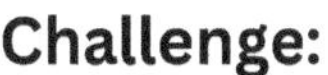

**Challenge:**
Take a photo of your child with
a statue of an animal that lives in the savannah.

Date:                          Location:

Today's
weather    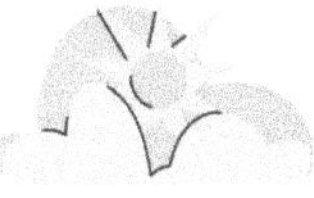  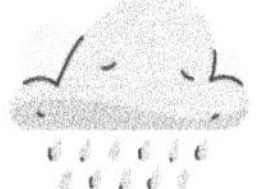 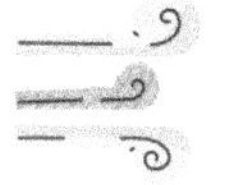 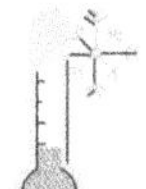

How many
people?    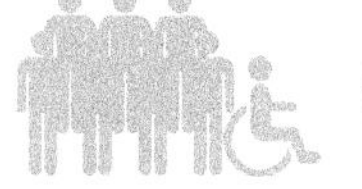 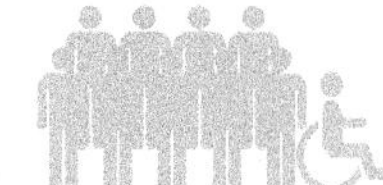

Would you rather be a lion or a hyena?

Where would you live, if you were a savannah animal?

What piece of play equipment do you think a lion would like to
play with? Why?

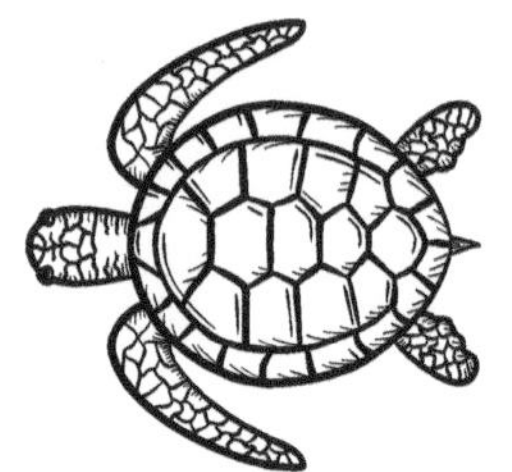 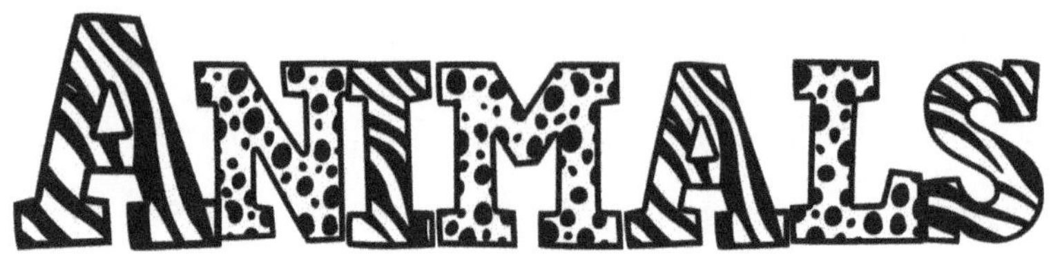

# ANIMALS

**Challenge:**
Take a photo of your child with
a statue of an animal that swims in the ocean.

Date:                          Location:

Today's
weather
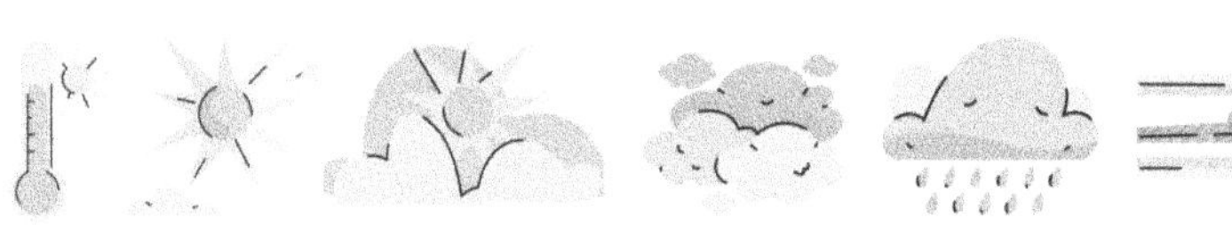

How many
people?
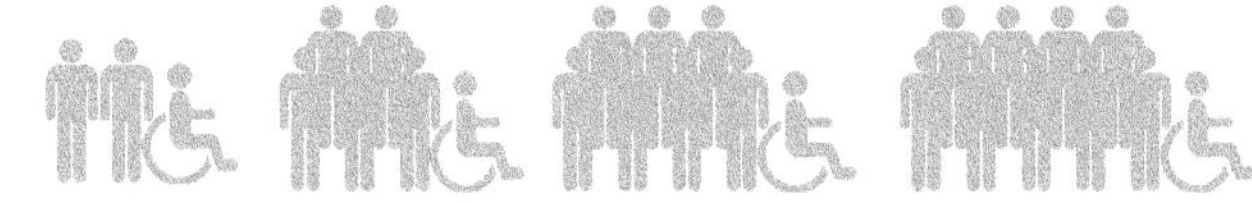

What ocean animal is your favourite? Why?

If you could be any type of fish, which would you choose?

Would you rather swim with dolphins, or swim with turtles?

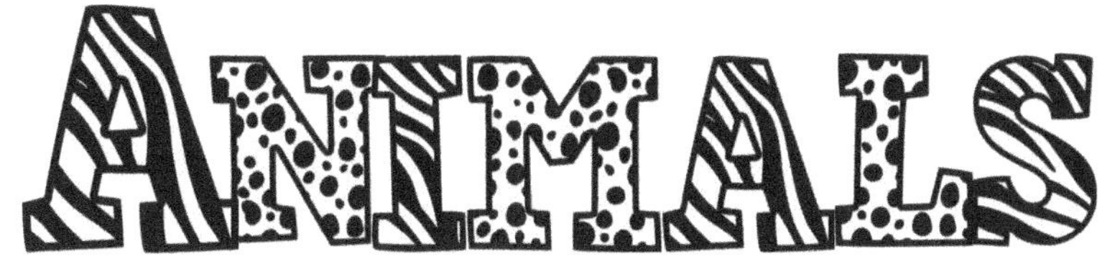
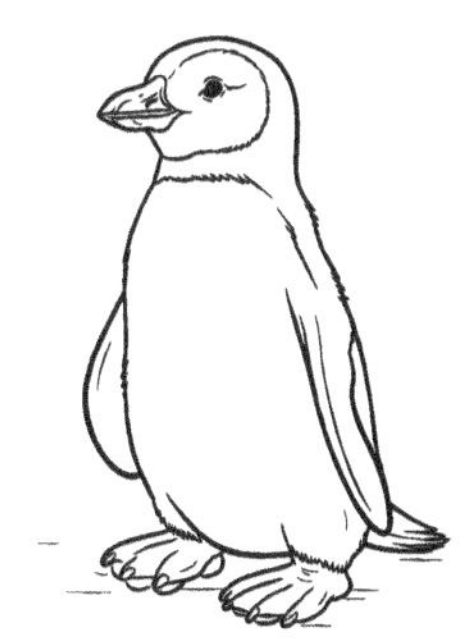

**Challenge:**
Take a photo of your child with
a statue of an animal that lives on snow or ice.

Date:                              Location:

Today's
weather          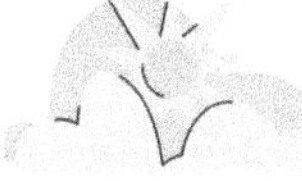 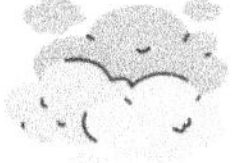 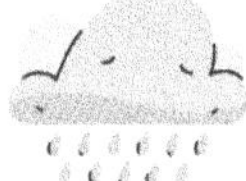 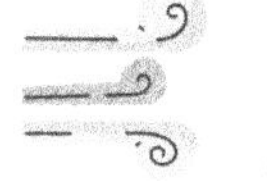 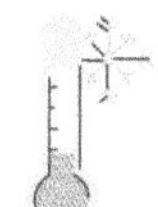

How many
people?          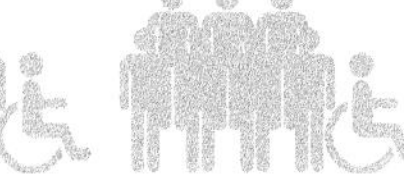 

Where would you rather live, on the ice or in snow?

If you could be a penguin or a polar bear, which would you be?

What would your animal prefer to play on at this park?

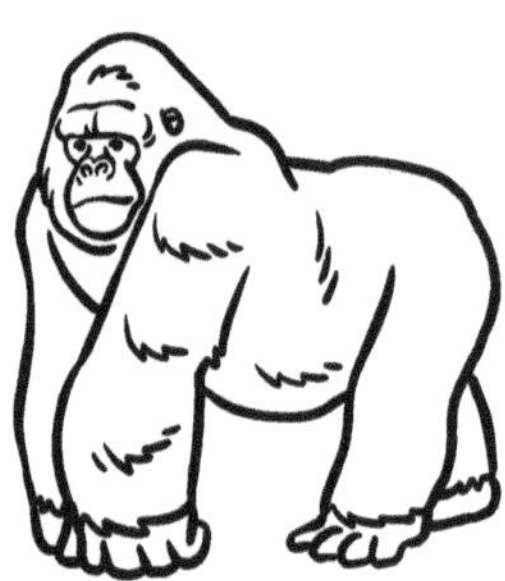 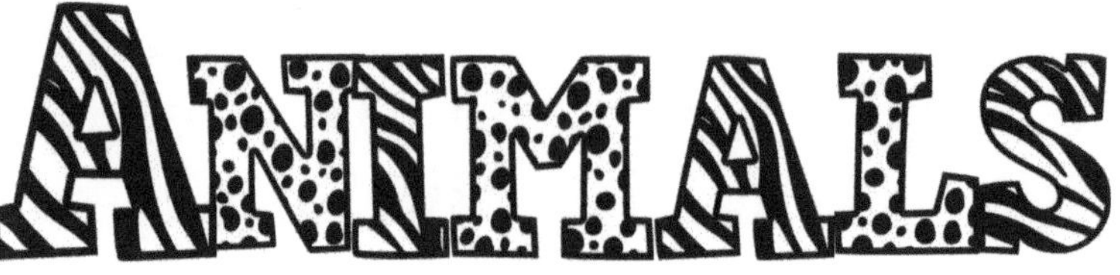

**Challenge:**
Take a photo of your child with
a statue of an animal that lives in the jungle.

Date:                    Location:

Today's
 weather

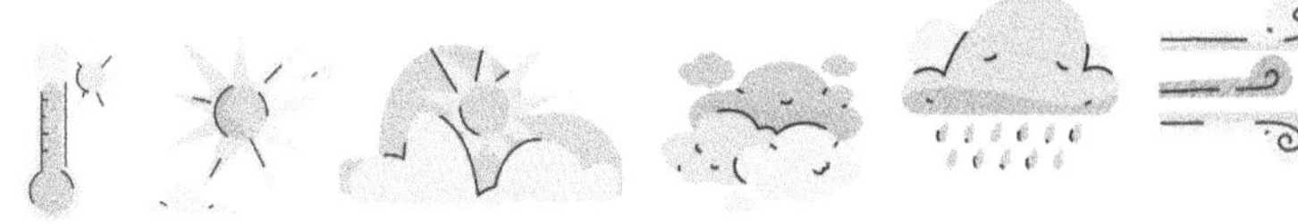

How many
people?

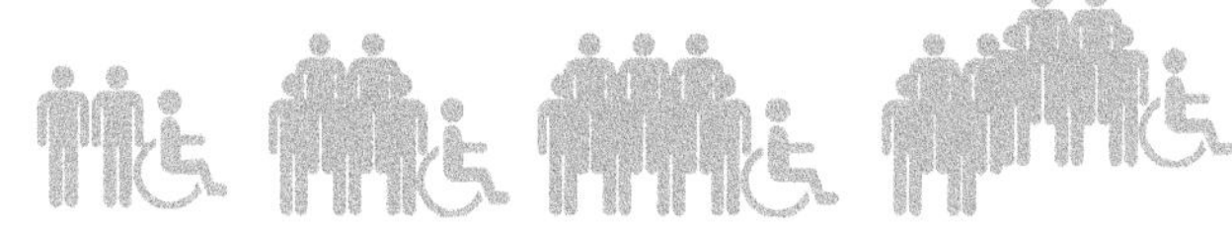

Would you rather live in the trees or on the jungle floor?


Which animal is your favourite jungle animal? Why?


Where would you find friends if you were a jungle animal??

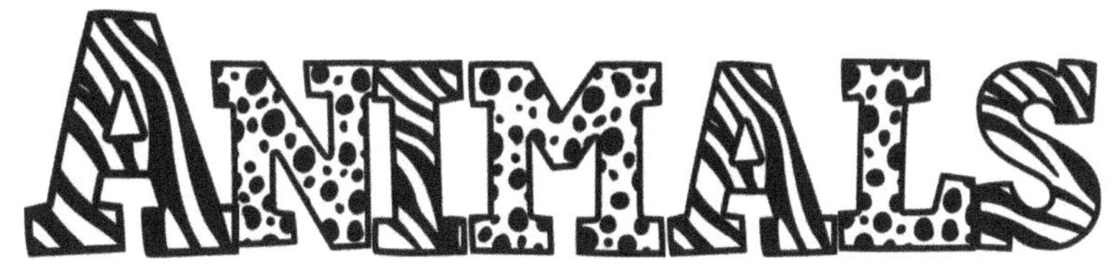

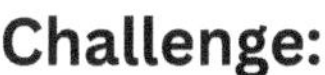

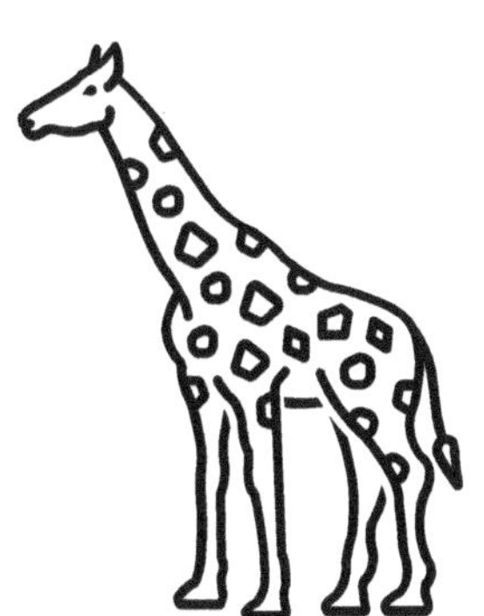

**Challenge:**
Take a photo of your child with
a statue of an animal that is taller than them.

Date:                    Location:

Today's
weather      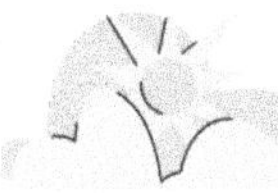 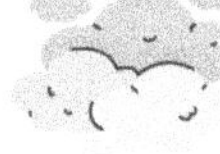 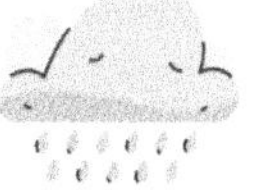 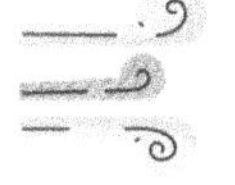 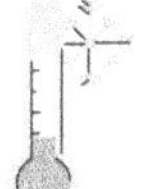

How many
people?

Would you rather have a long neck, or very long legs?

If you had to be a giraffe or a zebra, which would you choose? Why?

Where would you hide your favourite things, if you were super tall?:

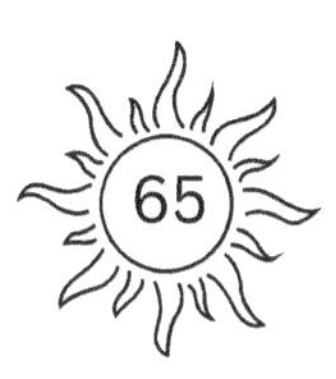

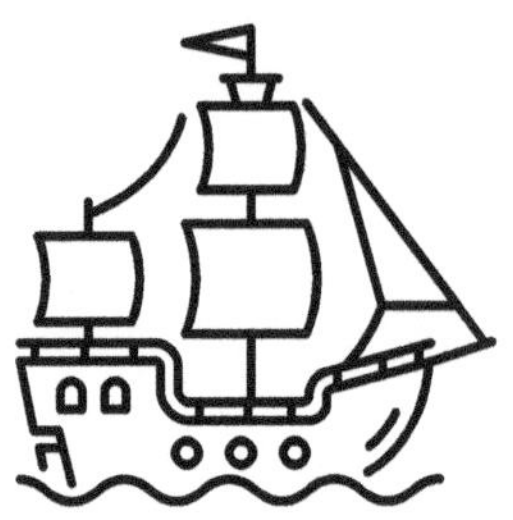

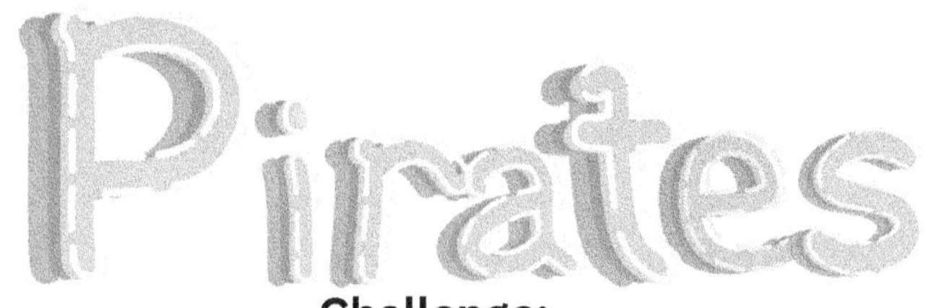


**Challenge:**

Take a photo of your child on a pirate ship.

Date:                          Location:

Today's weather

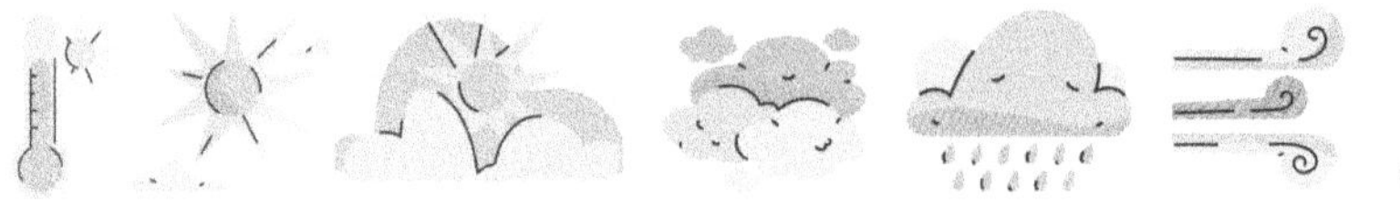

How many people?

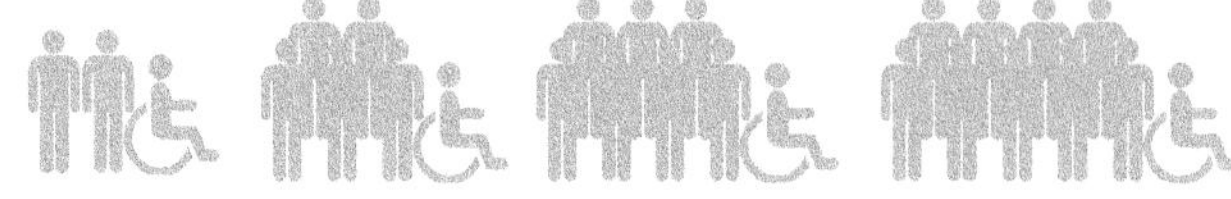

If you were the ships captain, what would you name your pirate ship?


Would you rather have a very large ship with big canons, or a small fast ship?


Where would you sail to on your pirate ship?

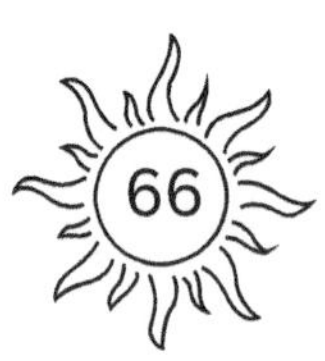

# 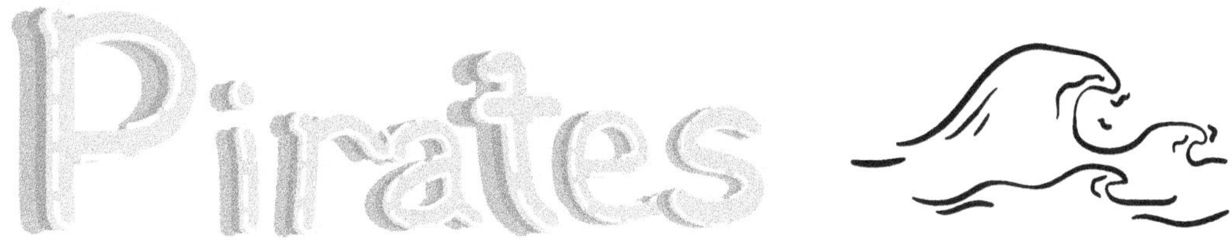 Pirates

**Challenge:**
Take a photo of your child at the first sea (a park beginning
with the letter C).

Date:                          Location:

Today's
weather

How many
people?

Can you name all of the seven seas?

If you could name an ocean, what would you call it?

Where would you like your ocean to be?

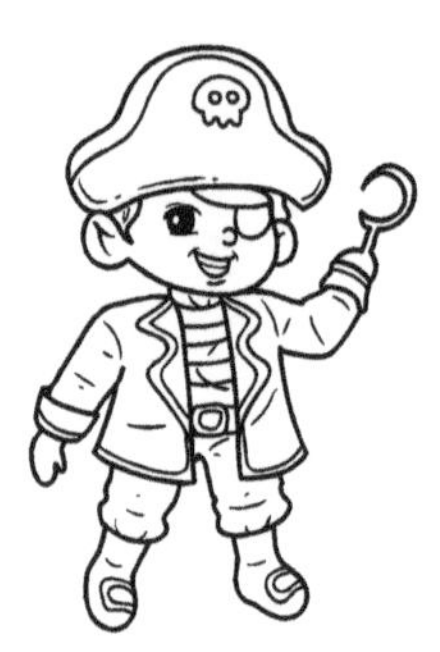

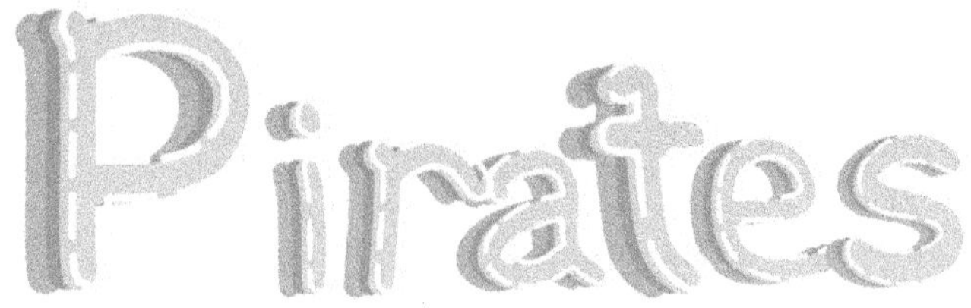


**Challenge:**
Take a photo of your child at the second sea (a park beginning with the letter C).

Date:                              Location:

Today's weather 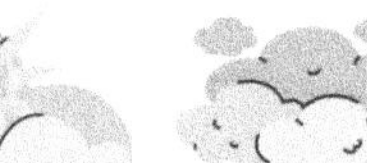 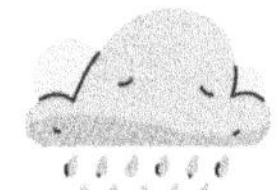  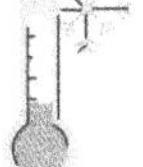

How many people? 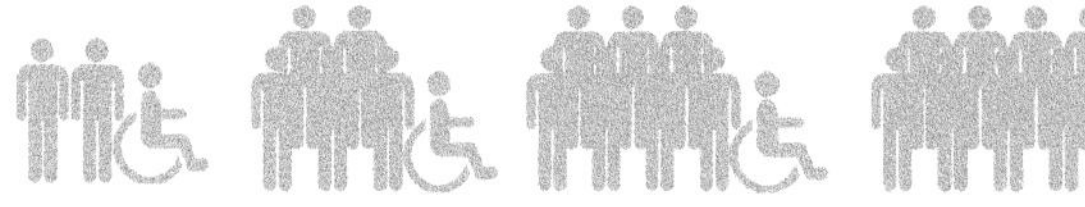

Would you rather have a peg for a leg, or a hook for a hand?

What colour would the sails of your pirate ship be? Why?

If you had a pirate pet which would you choose, a parrot or a monkey?

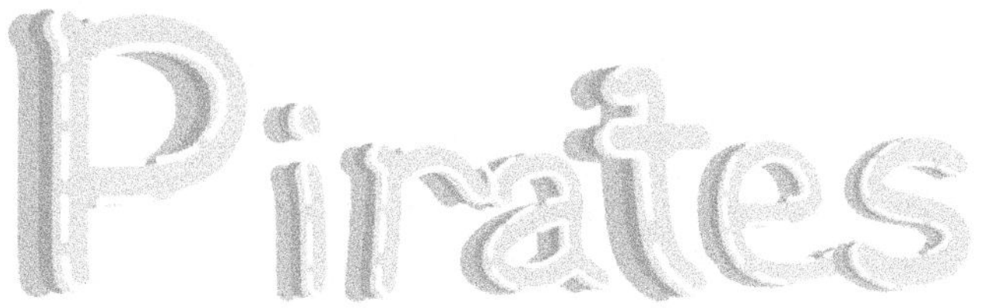
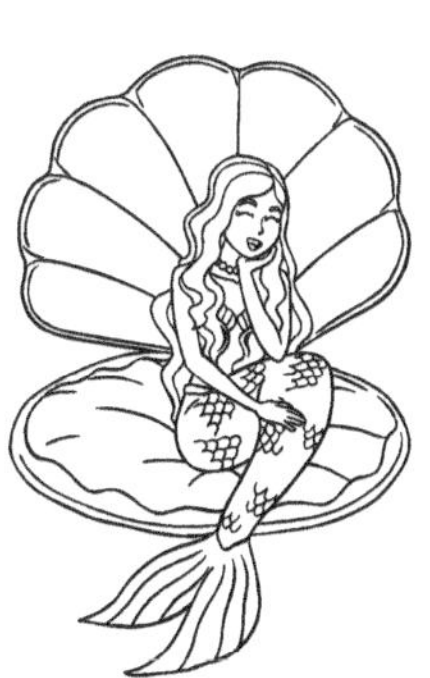

**Challenge:**
Take a photo of your child at the third sea (a park beginning
with the letter C).

Date:                              Location:

Today's
 weather      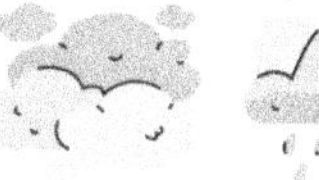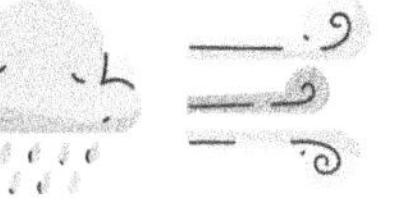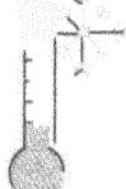

How many
people?

What would be your pirate name?


If you could be a pirate or a mermaid, which would you choose?


Where would you hide your ship, if someone was looking for you?

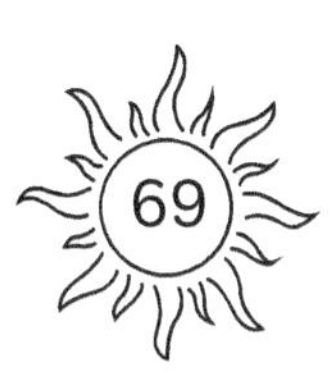

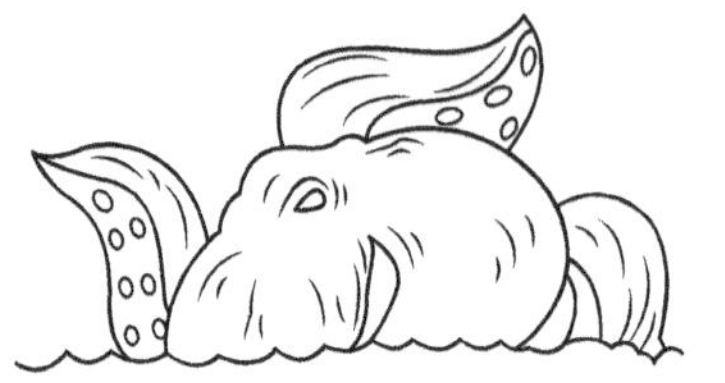 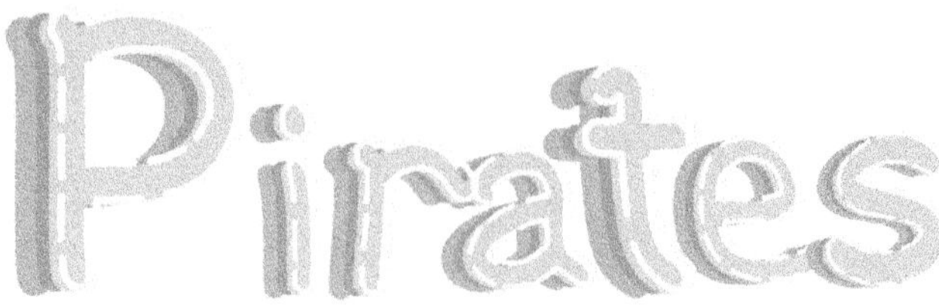

# Pirates

**Challenge:**
Take a photo of your child at the fourth sea (a park beginning with the letter C).

Date:                    Location:

Today's
weather 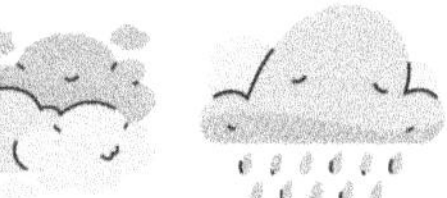 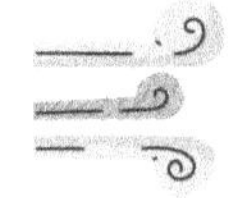 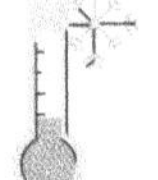

How many
people? 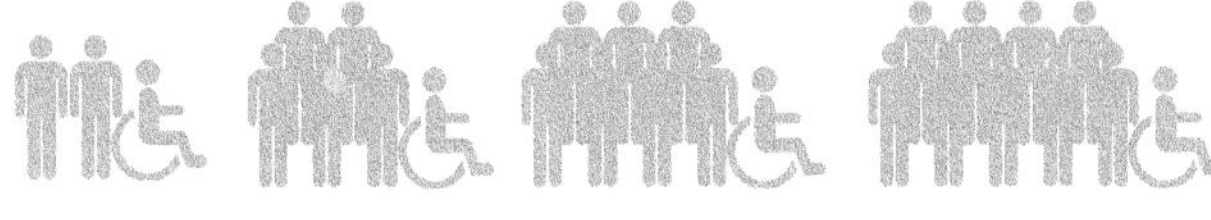

What things do you think pirates are afraid of? Are you afraid of anything?

If you found a sea monster, what would you do?

If you could have a pet sea monster, what would you pick?

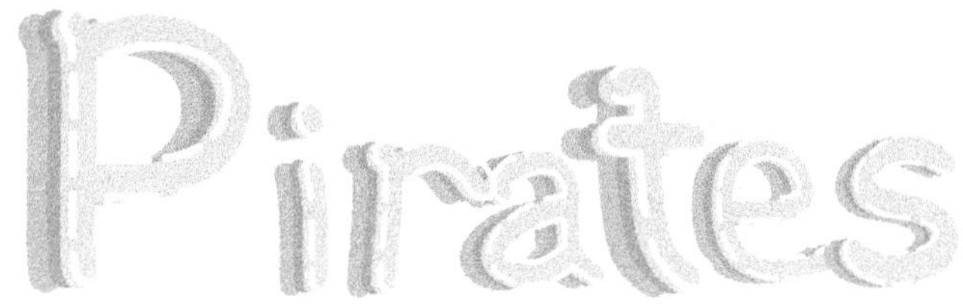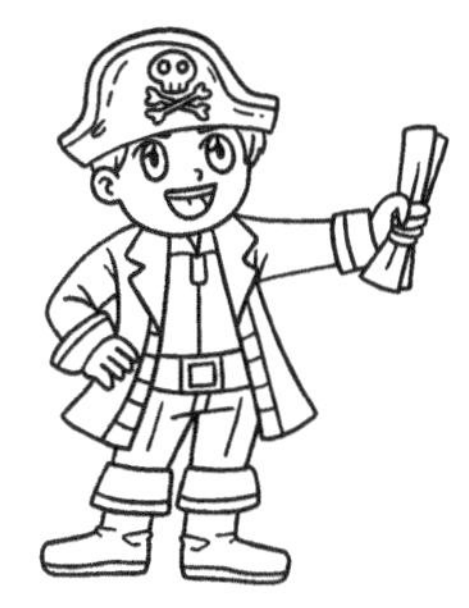

# Pirates

**Challenge:**
Take a photo of your child at the fifth sea (a park beginning with the letter C).

Date:                    Location:

Today's weather

How many people?

What would your flag look like on your pirate ship?

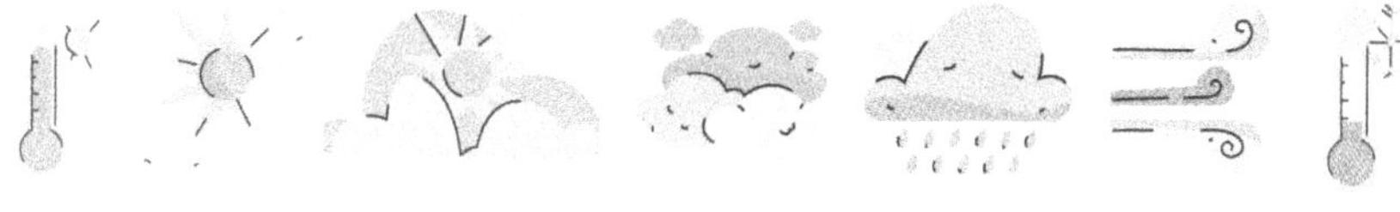

Who would be apart of your pirate crew, on your pirate ship?

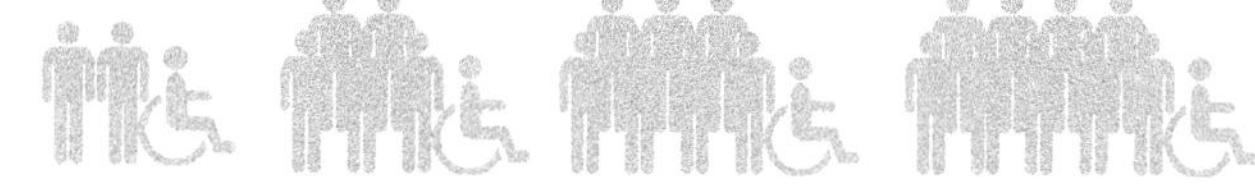

Which friend would be your 'first mate'? Why?

 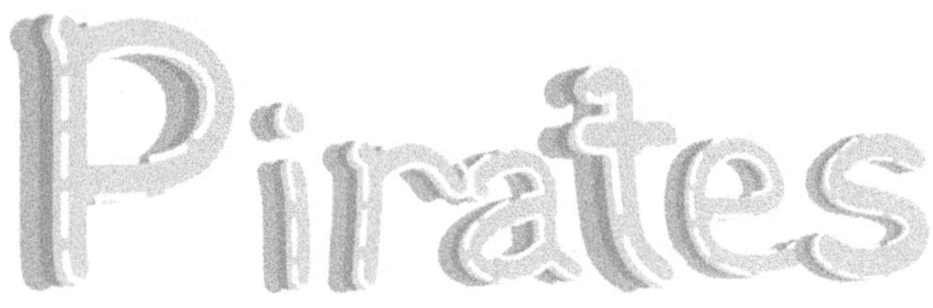

**Challenge:**
Take a photo of your child at the sixth sea (a park beginning
with the letter C).

Date:                    Location:

Today's
weather 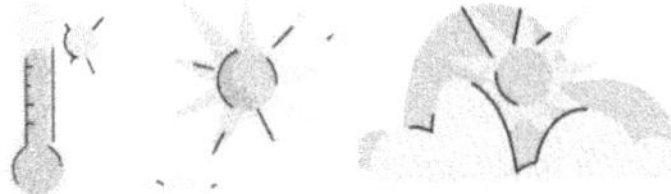 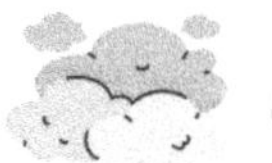 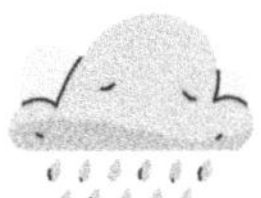 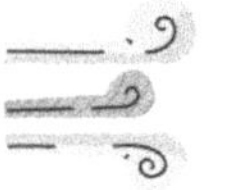 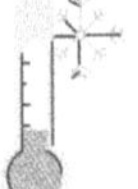

How many
people? 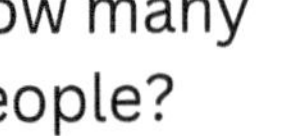 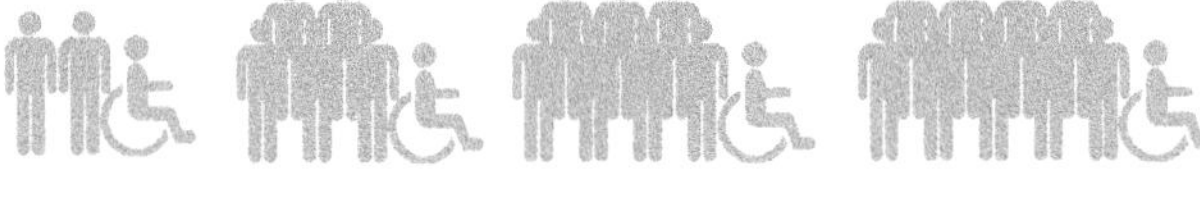

What pirate words or phrases do you know?




Would you rather have a sword fight holding one sword or two swords?




Where would you live as a pirate when you were not sailing your ship?

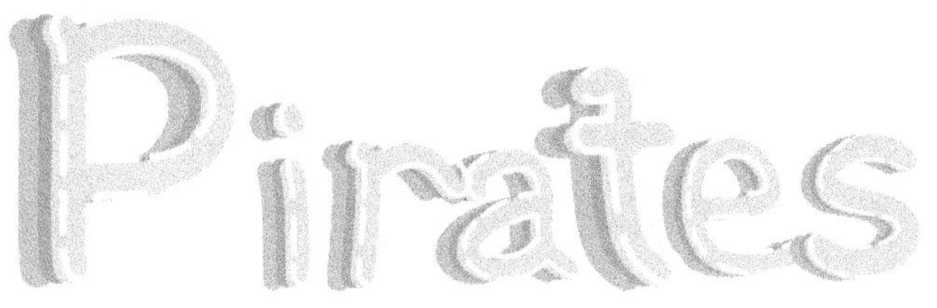
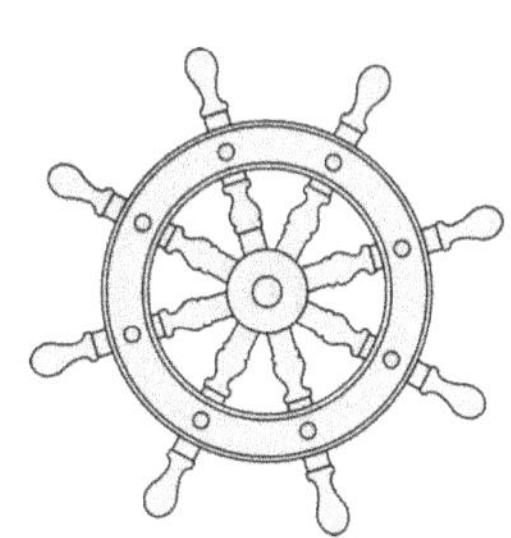

**Challenge:**
Take a photo of your child at the seventh sea (a park beginning with the letter C).

Date:                     Location:

Today's
weather
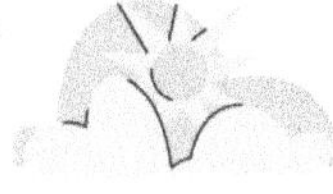 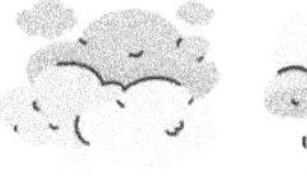 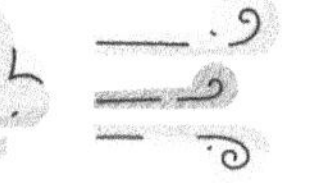 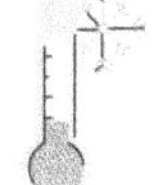

How many
people?
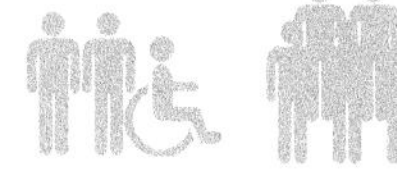 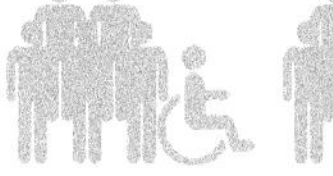 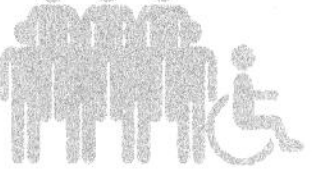 

What would be a pirates favourite part of this playground?

Would you rather climb the ships rope ladders, or steer the ship?

If you could choose a parent to be your 'first mate', who would you choose? Why?

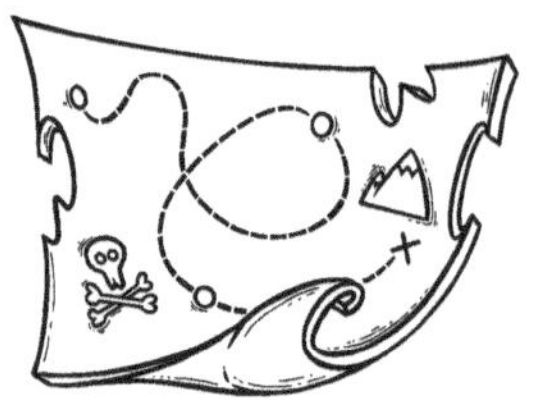 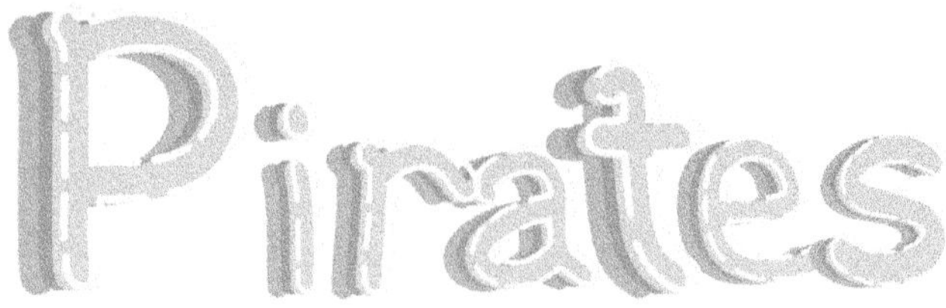

**Challenge:**
Take a photo of your child with their greatest treasure at a playground.

Date:                          Location:

Today's
weather
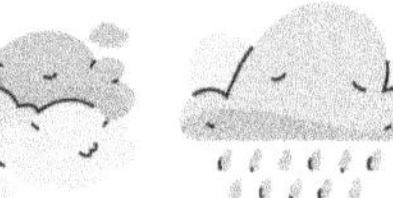 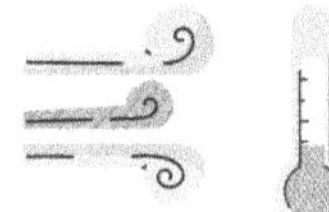 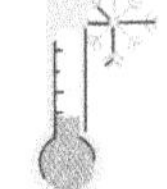

How many
people?
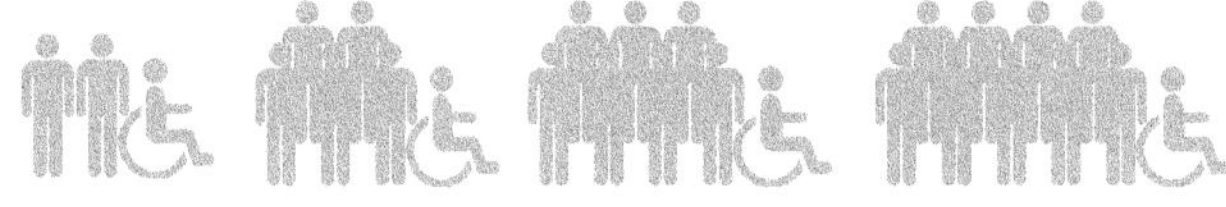

What kind of treasure would you lock in your treasure chest?


Where would you hide your treasure chest?


If you were to make a treasure map, who would you trust to look after it?

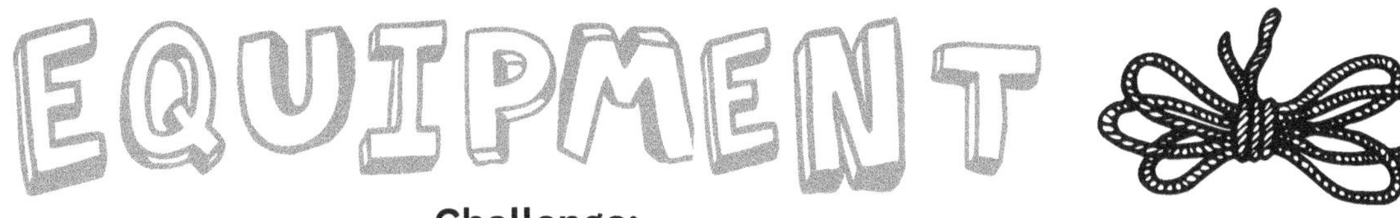

# EQUIPMENT

**Challenge:**
Take a photo of your child with
a piece of equipment  that is made from rope.

Date:                              Location:

Today's
 weather 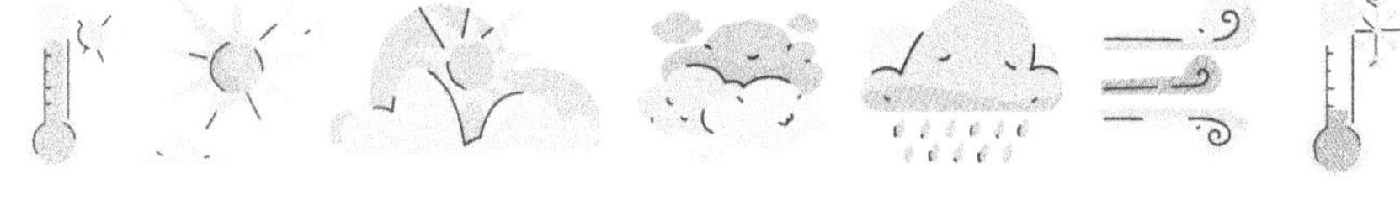

How many
people? 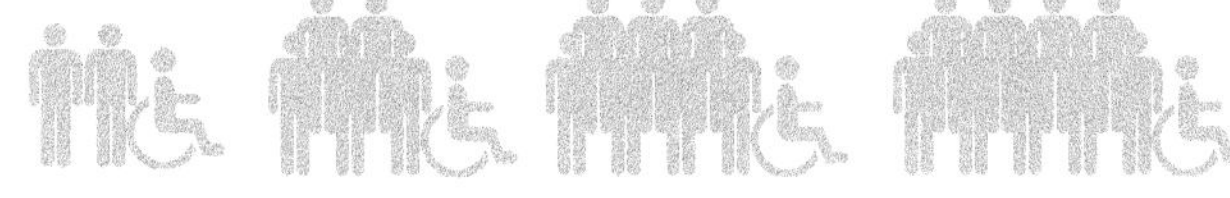

What made you laugh at this playground?


Would you ask a friend to come to this playground with you?


If you could design a rope piece of equipment, what would it look like?

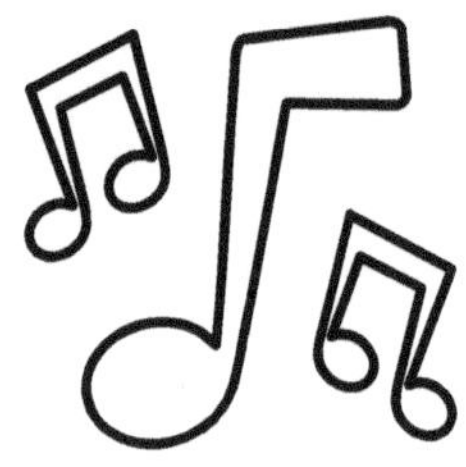
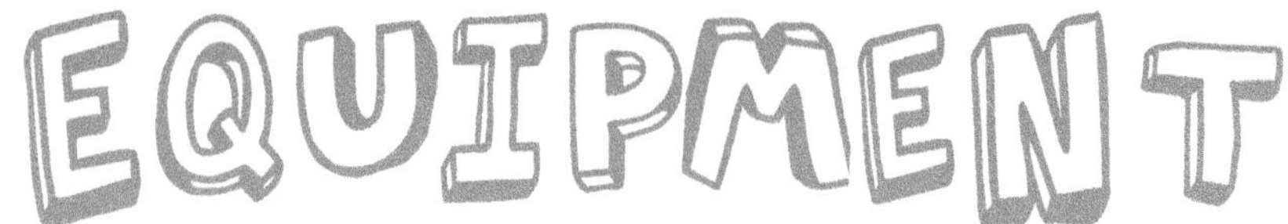

# EQUIPMENT

**Challenge:**
Take a photo of your child with
a piece of equipment that makes sound/music.

Date:                    Location:

Today's
weather
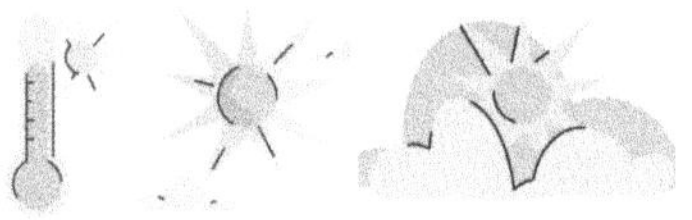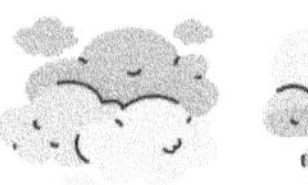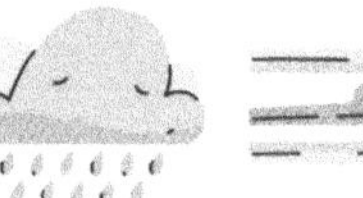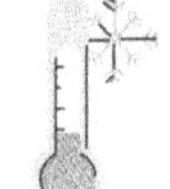

How many
people?
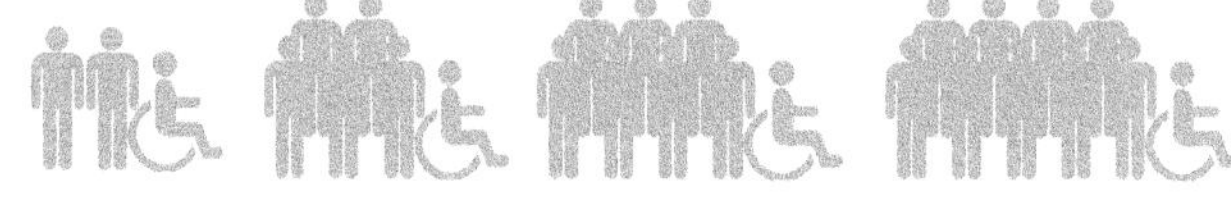

What is your favourite musical instrument? Why?

Which instrument would you like to learn to play?

Do you like making music with a friend better, or on your own?

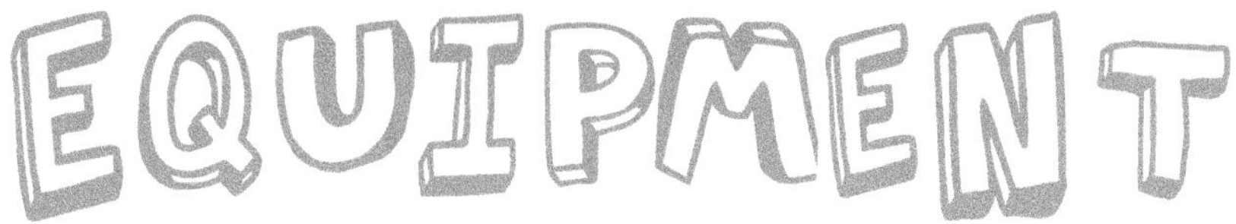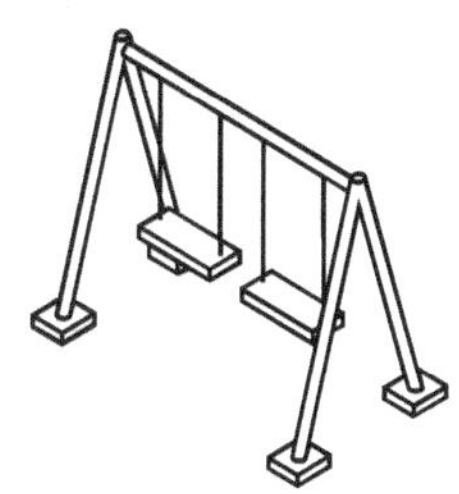

# EQUIPMENT

**Challenge:**
Take a photo of your child with
a piece of equipment that they can swing on.

Date:                    Location:

Today's
weather

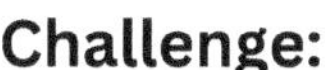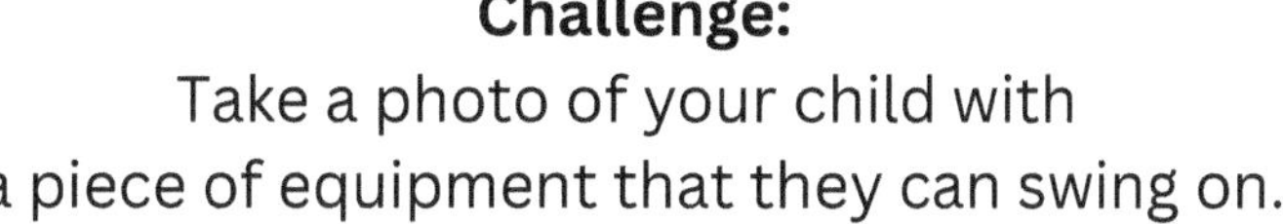

How many
people?

Do you like swinging really high or smaller swings?

Would you rather swing over water or over lots of flowers?

Who do you think can swing the highest out of your parents?

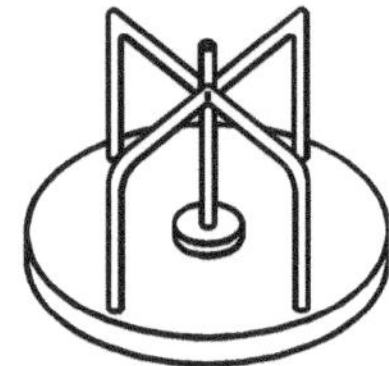



**Challenge:**
Take a photo of your child with
a piece of equipment that spins.

Date:              Location:

Today's
weather
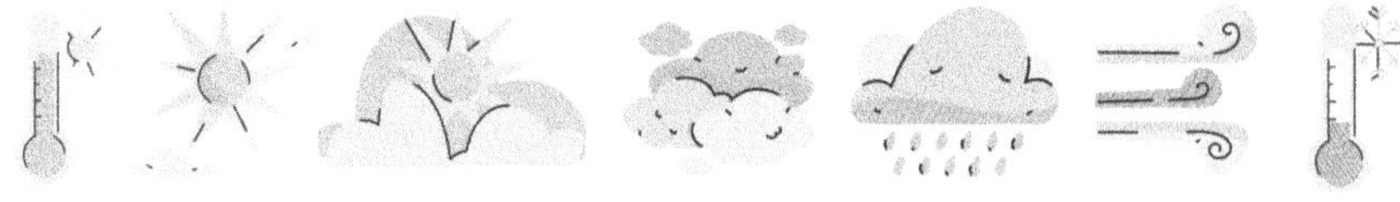

How many
people?
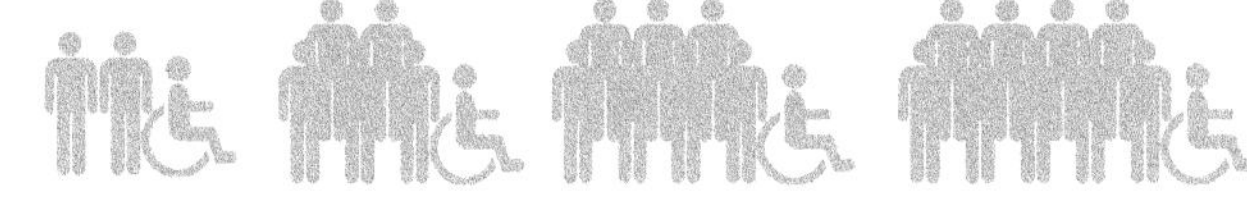

Do you like to spin fast or to spin slowly?

Which if your favourite type of spinning equipment? Why?

Would you rather spin yourself or have someone else spin you?

# 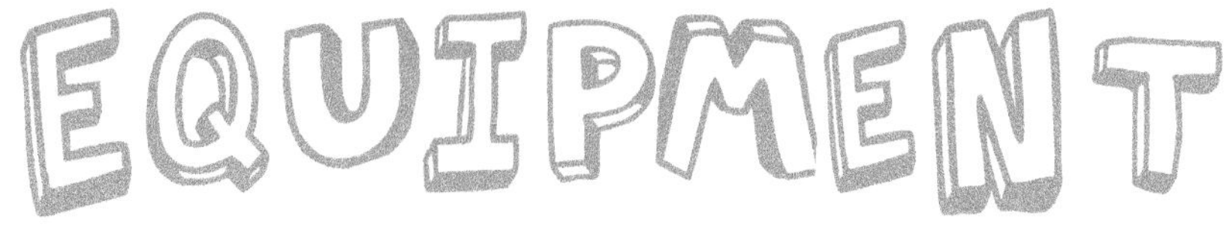 EQUIPMENT

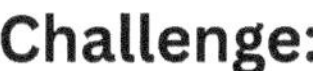

**Challenge:**
Take a photo of your child with
a piece of equipment made with chains.

Date:                          Location:

Today's
weather 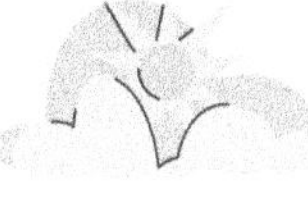 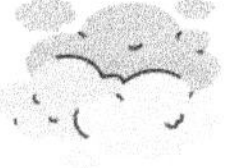 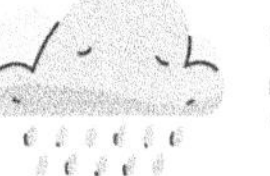 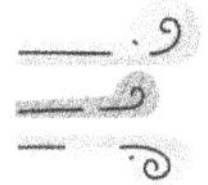 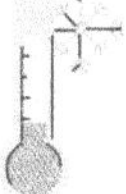

How many
people? 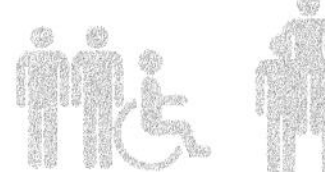 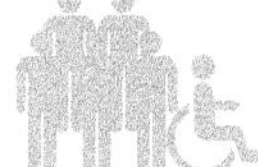 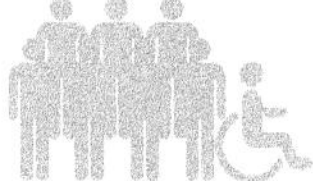 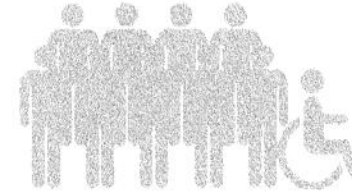

What did you like the most about this piece of equipment?

Would you want equipment like this at your home so you can play with
it everyday?

If you could build something out of chains, what would you build?

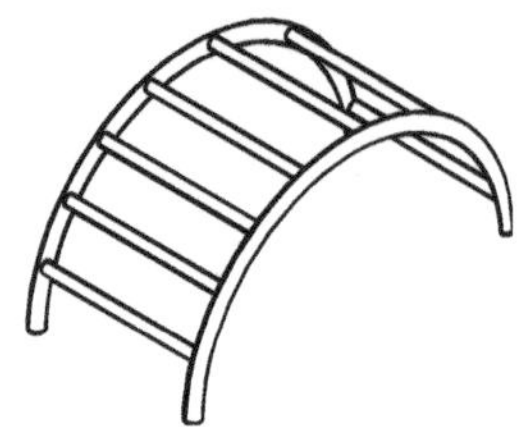

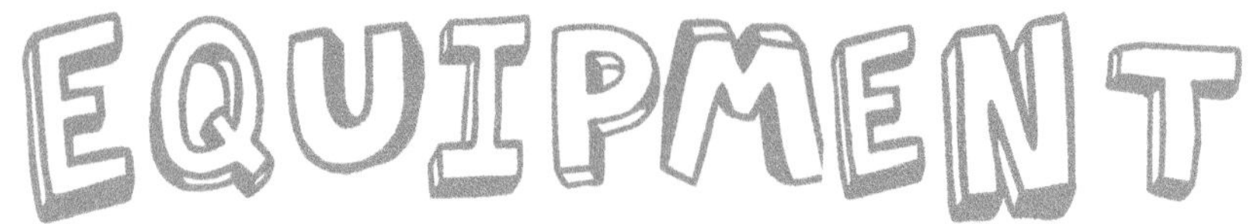
# EQUIPMENT

**Challenge:**
Take a photo of your child with
a piece of equipment that is used for climbing.

Date:                              Location:

Today's
weather
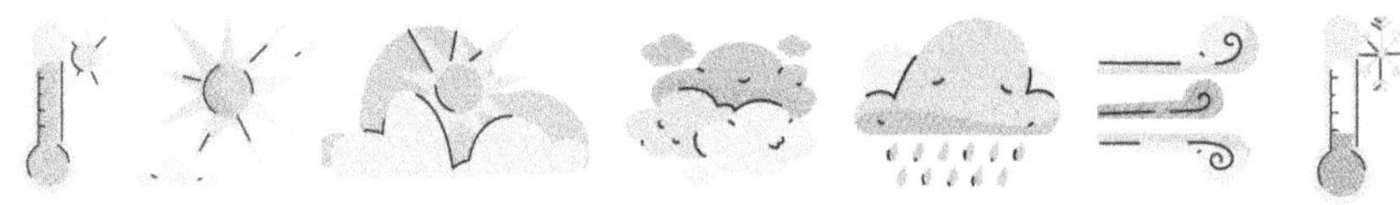

How many
people?
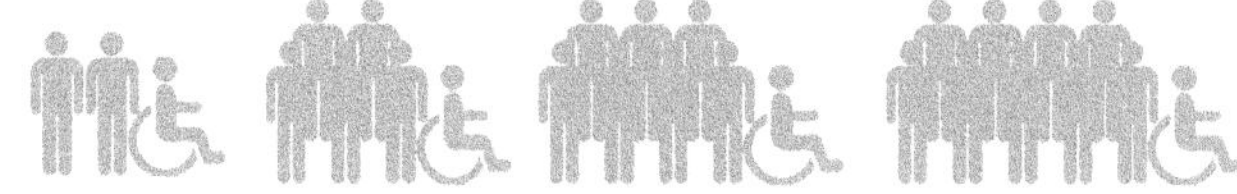

What material is this made from? Do you know where it comes from?

If you could climb anything, what would you choose to climb?

Would you rather climb up rocks or climb up a ladder?

# 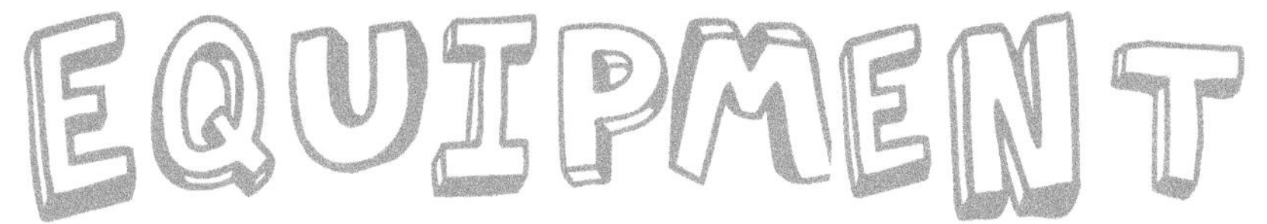 EQUIPMENT

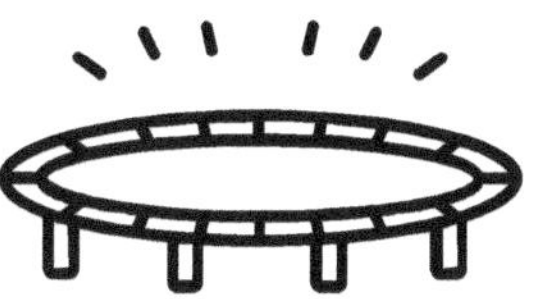

**Challenge**:
Take a photo of your child with
a piece of equipment that they can be bounced on.

Date:                    Location:

Today's
weather

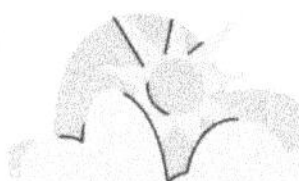 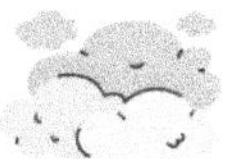 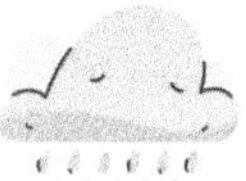 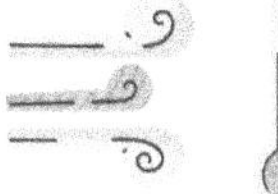 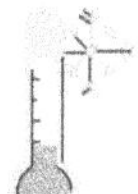

How many
people?

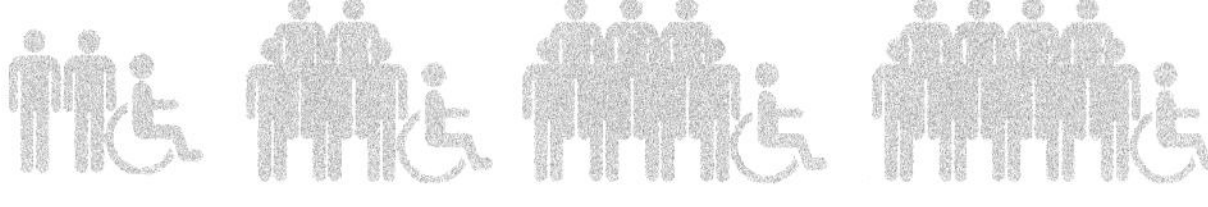

Do you enjoy being bounced or bouncing yourself?

Would you rather bounce really high or be bounced for a long time?

What was your favourite piece of equipment at this playground?

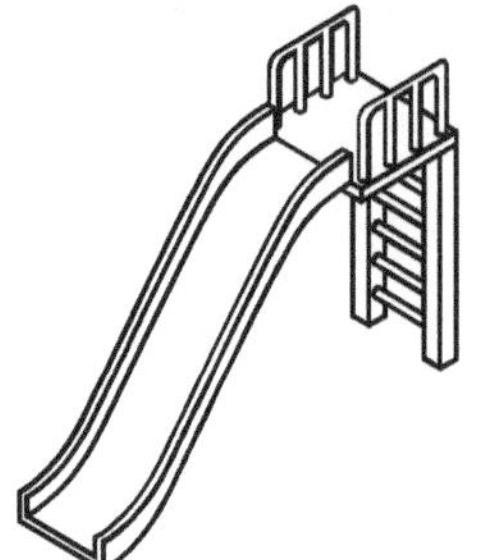 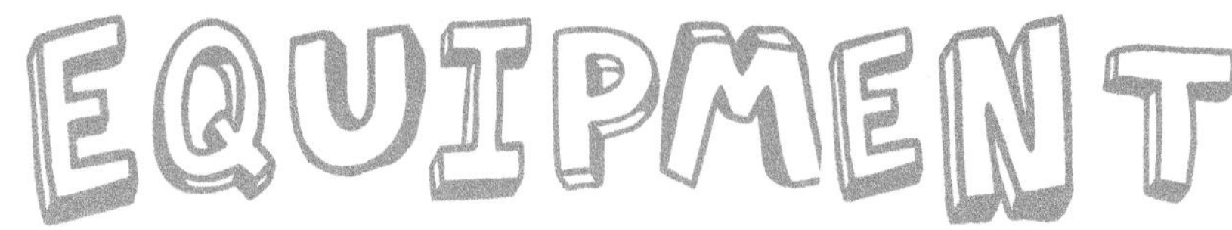

# EQUIPMENT

**Challenge:**
Take a photo of your child with
a piece of equipment that they can slide on.

Date:                          Location:

Today's
weather     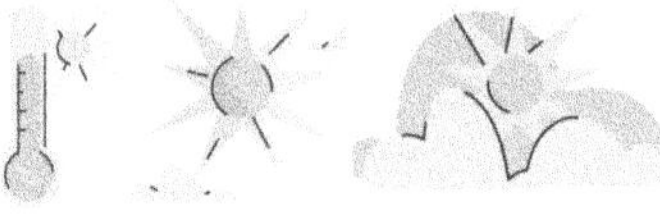 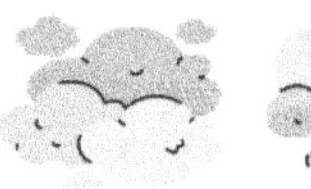  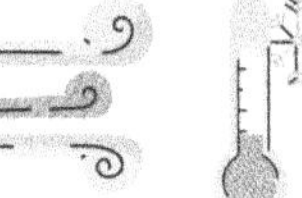 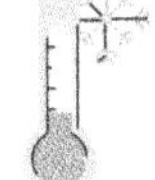

How many
people?     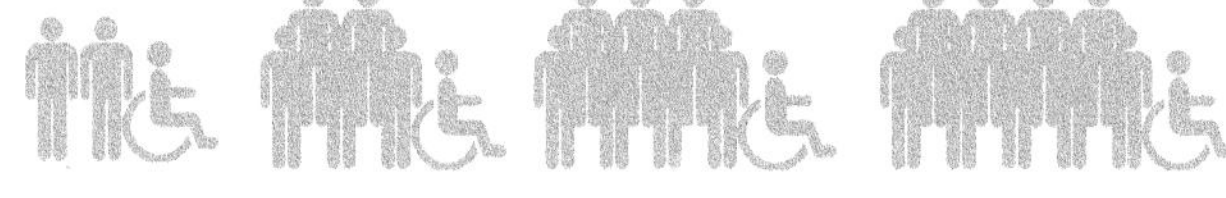

Which of your friends do you think would like this playground? Why?

Do you like slides that are open or tunnel slides better? Why?

Have you ever been on a water slide? Is that something you would want to
do/do again?

# 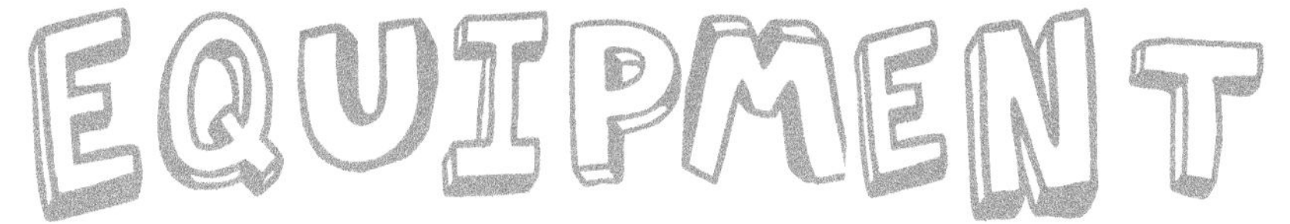 EQUIPMENT 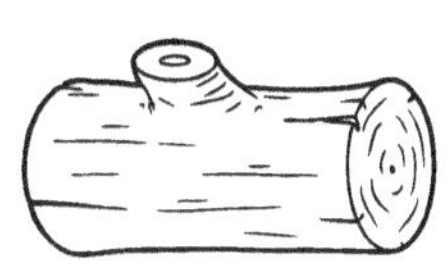

**Challenge:**
Take a photo of your child with
a piece of equipment made from wood.

Date:                    Location:

Today's
 weather   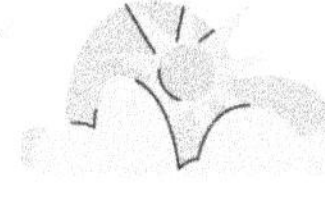 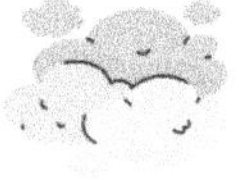 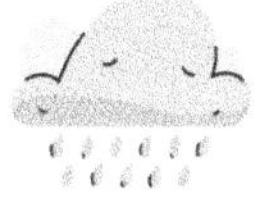 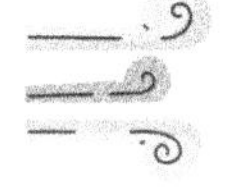 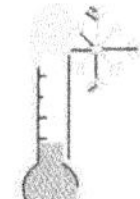

How many
people?   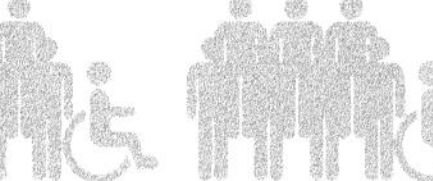 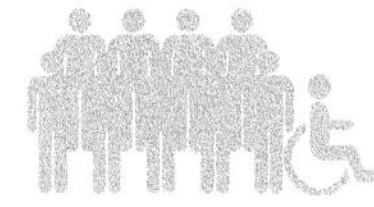

Where is your favourite hiding place at this playground?


Do you think your parents could build this type of equipment? Why/why not?


Which material do you like better, wood or plastic? Why?

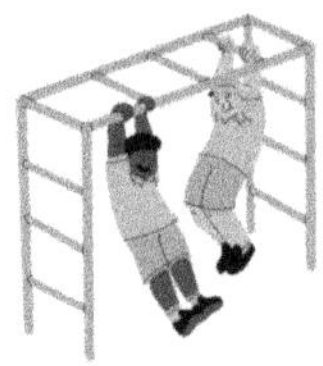

# 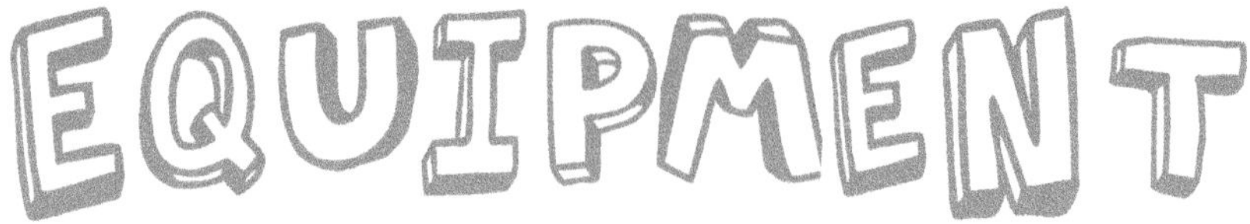EQUIPMENT

**Challenge**:
Take a photo of your child with
a piece of equipment that needs to be held to be used.

Date:                    Location:

Today's
weather 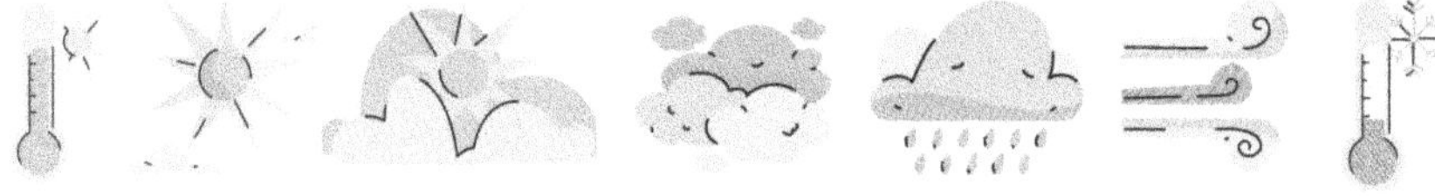

How many
people? 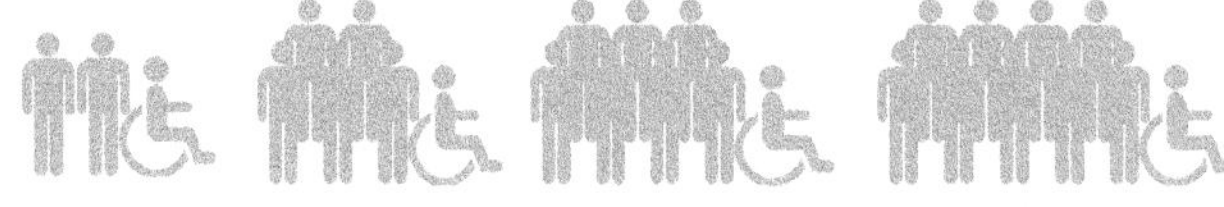

How old do you think this playground is? Do you know how to find the answer?

Do you prefer to go on a flying fox or monkey bars?

Who do you think can hang onto monkey bars the longest out of your family?

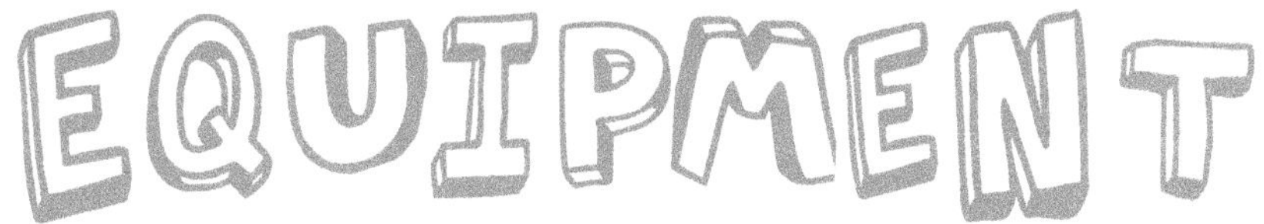# EQUIPMENT

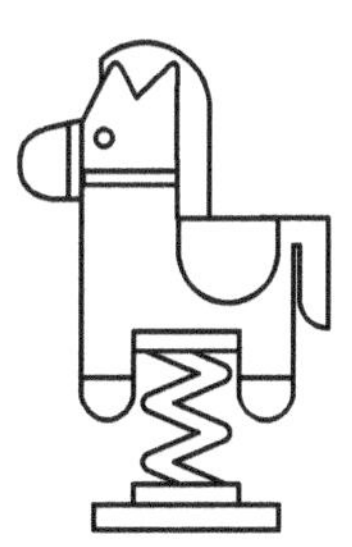

**Challenge:**
Take a photo of your child with
a piece of equipment that has a spring.

Date:                    Location:

Today's
 weather     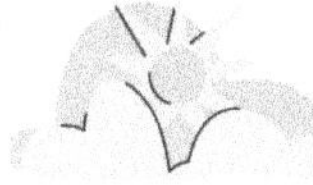 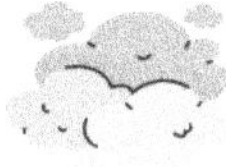 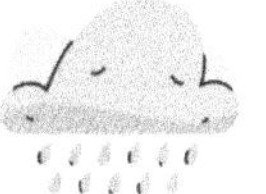 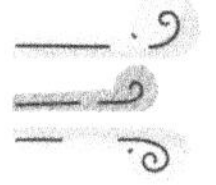 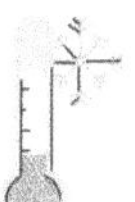

How many
people?     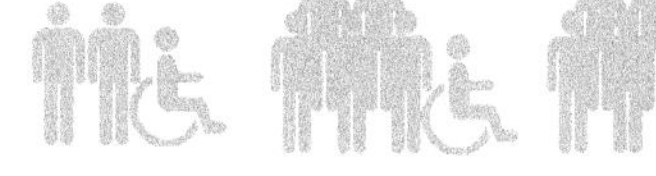 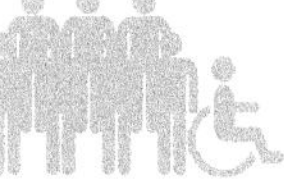 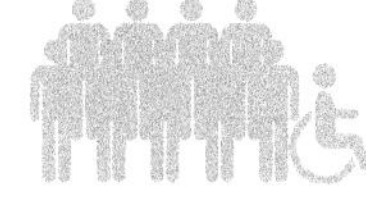

What is your favourite plant at this playground?


Which is your favourite of the pieces of equipment that come with a spring?


Who is your favourite person to go on a see saw with?

**Challenge:**
Take a photo of your child at a playground with
a mountain/hill in the background.

Date:                                    Location:

Today's
weather

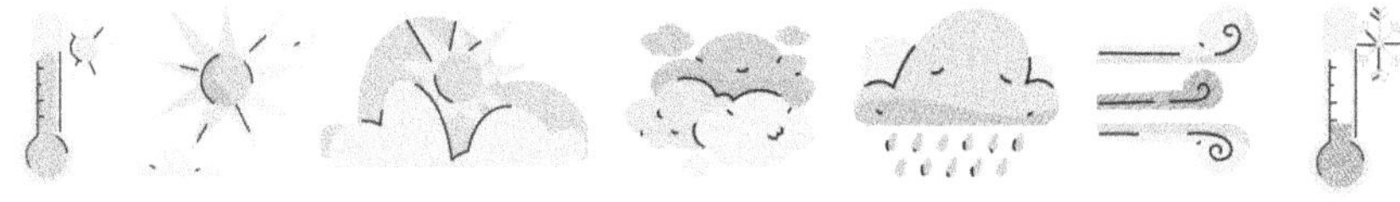

How many
people?

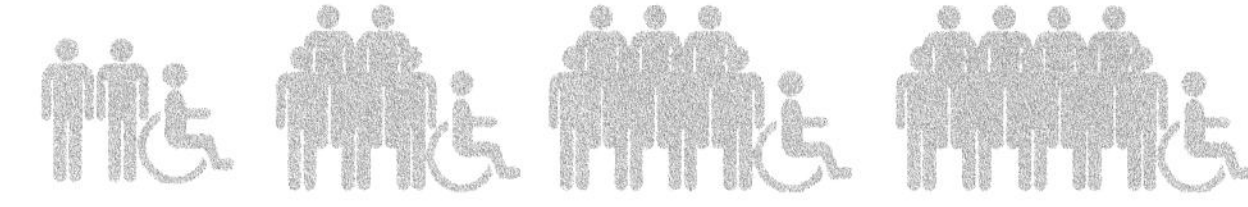

How do you think this hill/mountain was made?

Would you rather run up a hill or roll down a hill?

What types of animals do you think live on mountains?

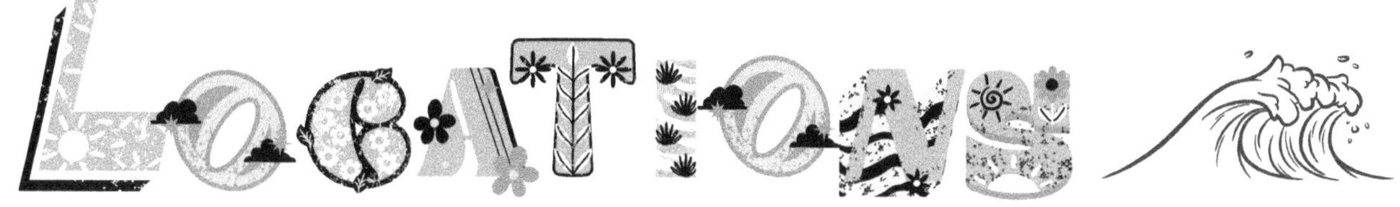



**Challenge:**
Take a photo of your child at a playground with
the ocean in the background.

Date:                     Location:

Today's
 weather

How many
people?

When is your favourite time to go swimming?

Do you prefer to swim in a pool or in the ocean?

What is your favourite ocean animal? Why?

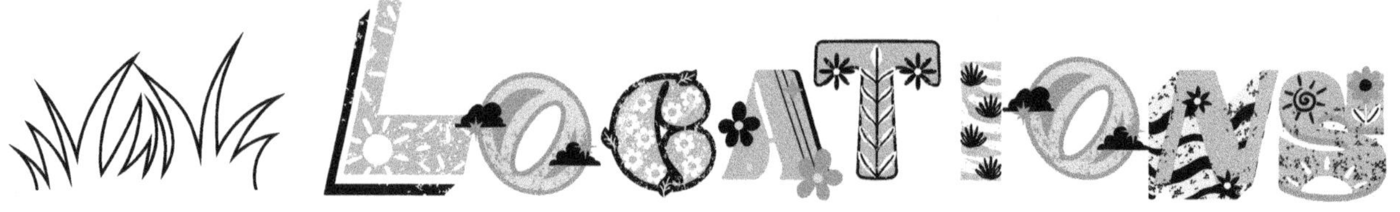


**Challenge:**
Take a photo of your child at a playground with
a grass field/oval in the background.

Date:                              Location:

Today's
weather 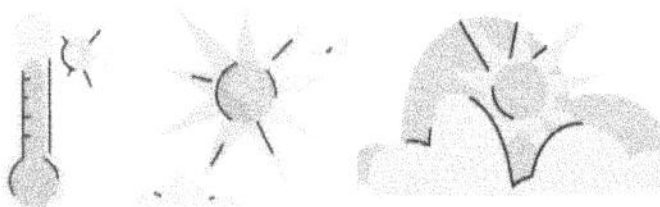 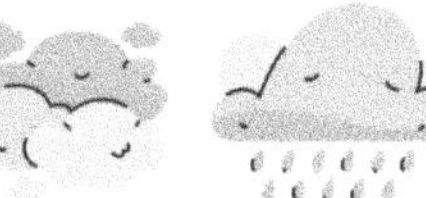 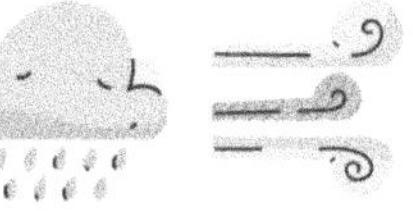 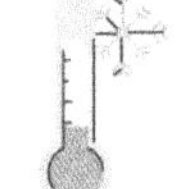

How many
people? 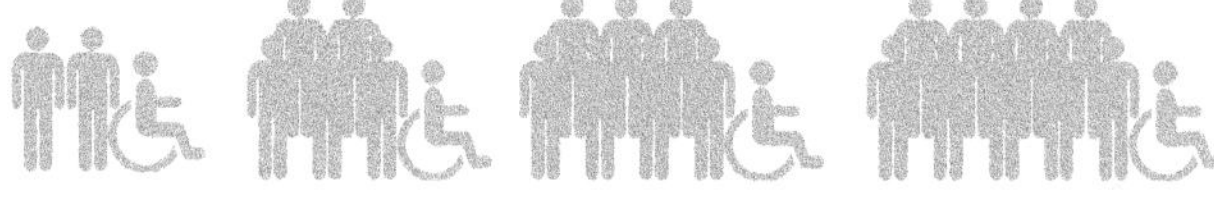

What is your favourite game/activity to play on the grass?

If you could choose a new colour for grass, what would it be?

Can you name the different types of bugs and animals that live in grass?

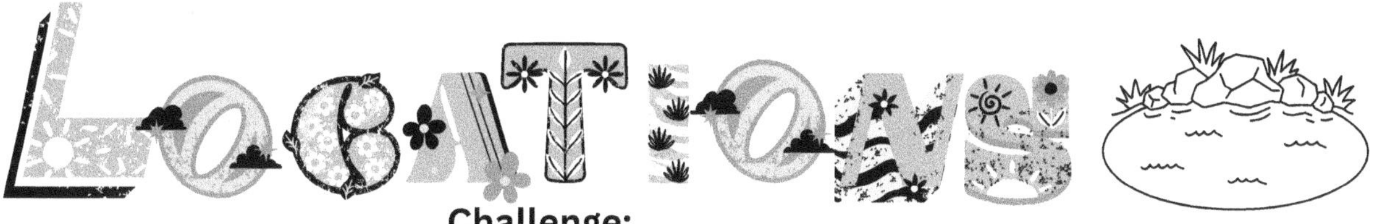

**Challenge:**
Take a photo of your child at a playground with
a lake in the background.

Date:                          Location:

Today's
 weather

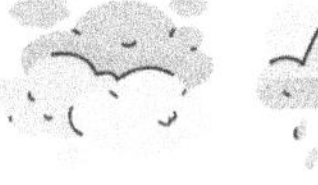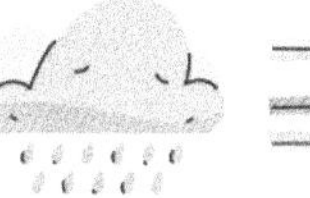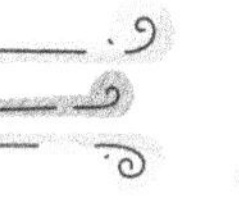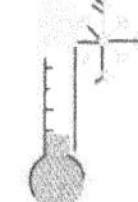

How many
people?

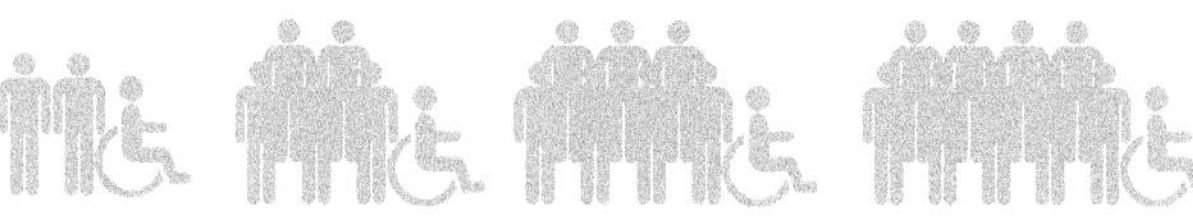

 What was your favourite moment at the playground today?

What types of animals do you think live in lakes?

Would you rather live near a lake or near a river?

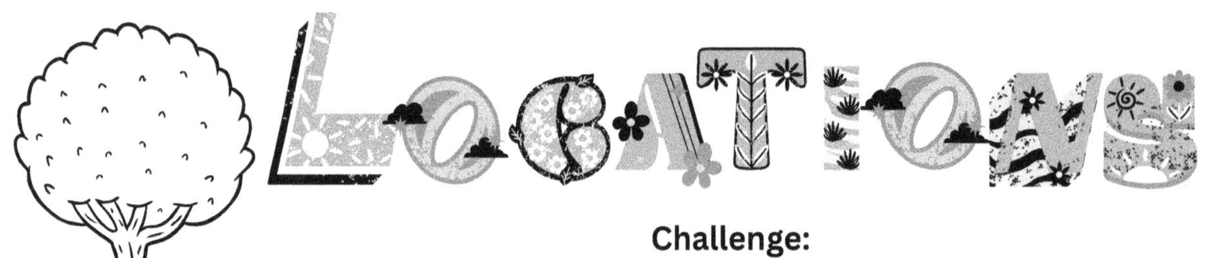


**Challenge:**
Take a photo of your child at a playground with
a large tree in the background.

Date:                              Location:

Today's
weather
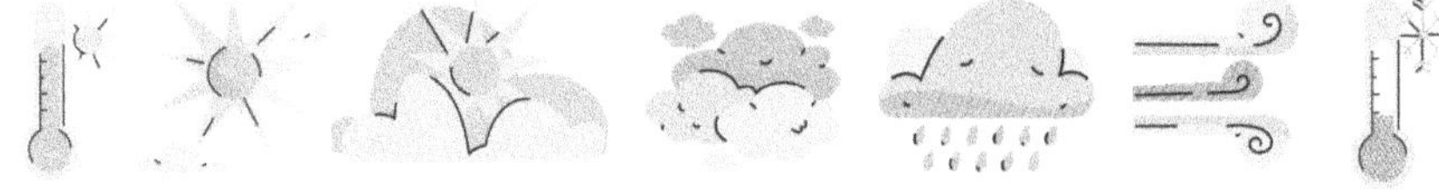

How many
people?
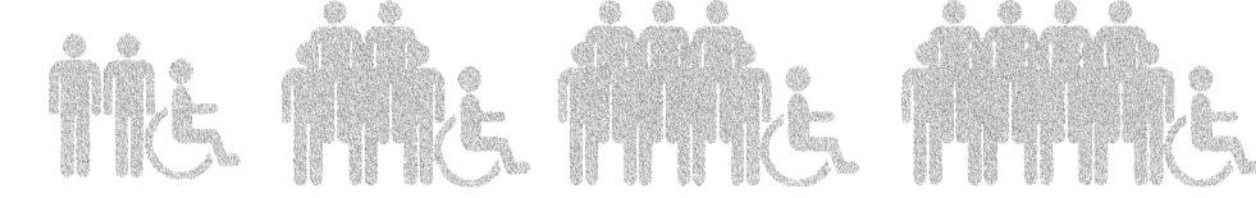

What is your favourite animal that lives in a tree? Why?

Would you rather climb a tree, or have a picnic under it?

If you could plant any type of tree, which one would you pick?

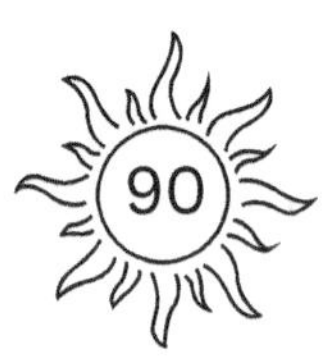

**Challenge:**
Take a photo of your child at a playground with
large boulders/rocks in the background.

Date:             Location:

Today's
weather

How many
people?

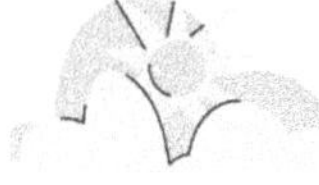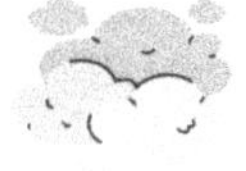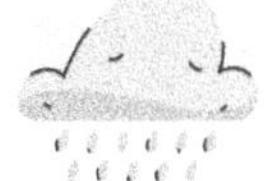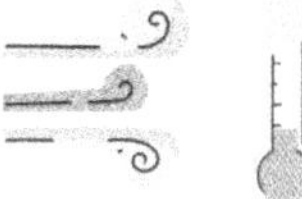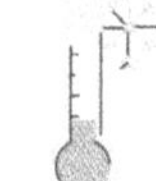

Do you think you could lift/move that rock/boulder? Why/why not?

If you could be any type of rock/stone, what would you be?

Where did that rock/boulder come from?

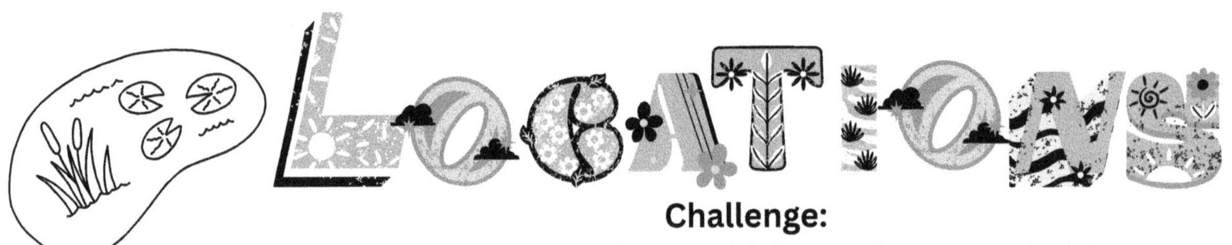

**Challenge:**
Take a photo of your child at a playground with
a pond in the background.

Date:                    Location:

Today's
weather
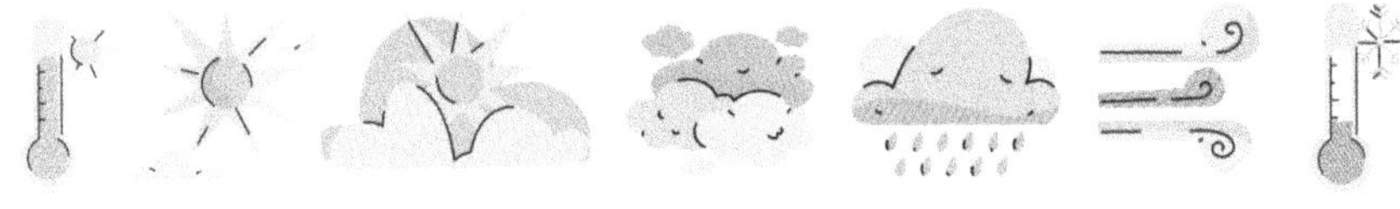

How many
people?
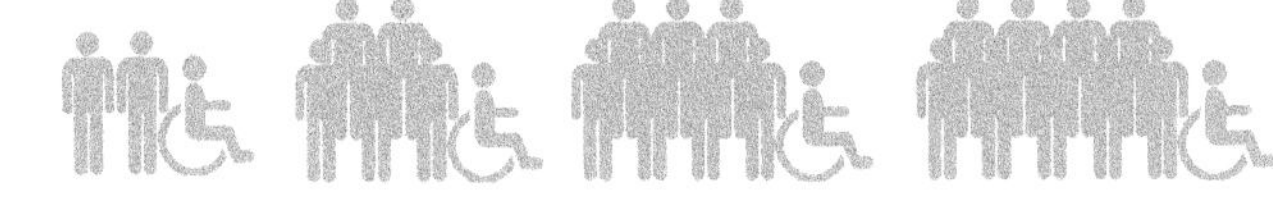

Would you come back to this playground?


What is your favourite animal that lives in a pond?


Where do you think animals that live in a pond go to sleep at night?

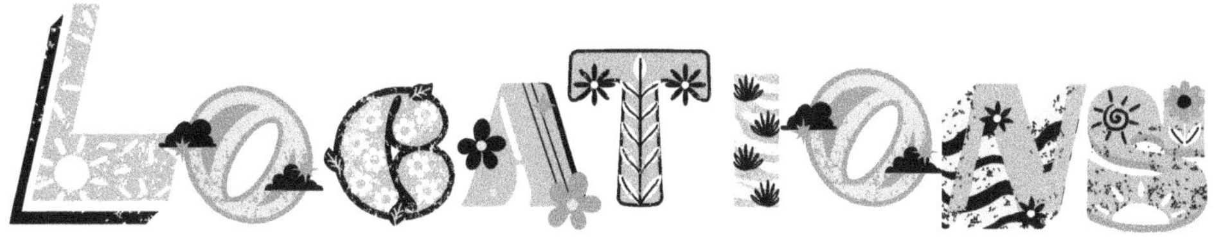

**Challenge:**
Take a photo of your child at a playground with
a forest/bush in the background.

Date:                          Location:

Today's
 weather

How many
people?

Who would you bring to play at this playground, if you were to come back?
Why that person?

 What is your favourite sculpture/structure that you have made from sticks?

Would you rather live in a forest or in bushland? Why?

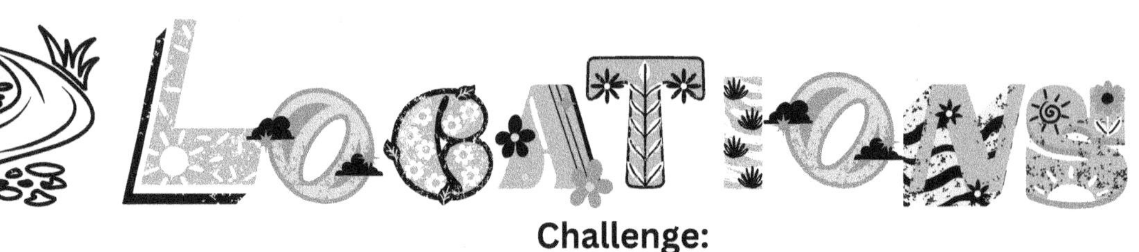

# Challenge:
Take a photo of your child at a playground with
a river in the background.

Date: Location:

Today's
weather 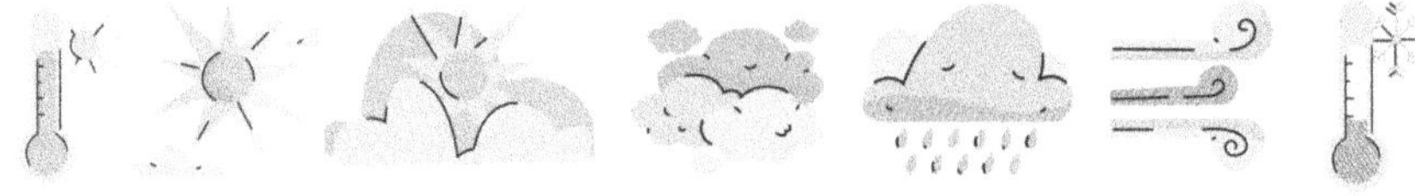

How many
people? 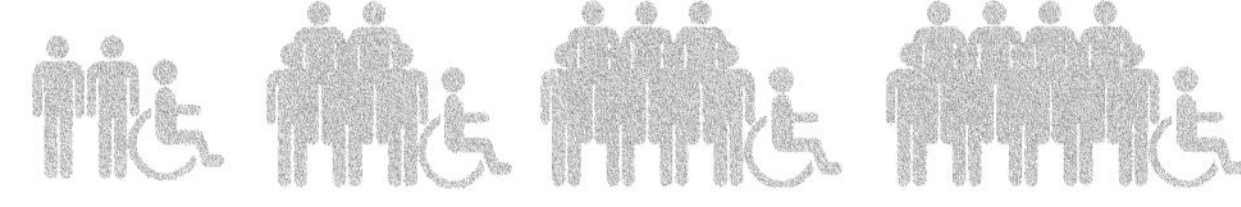

Who is your favourite person to go to a playground with?

If you could name this river, what would you name it?

Do you prefer rivers or beaches? Why?

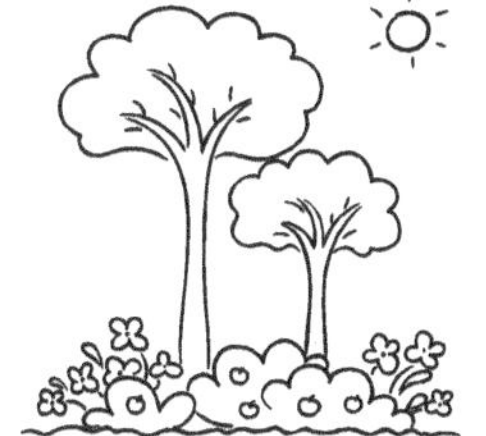

**Challenge:**
Take a photo of your child at a playground with
lots of flowers in the background.

Date: Location:

Today's weather 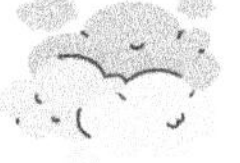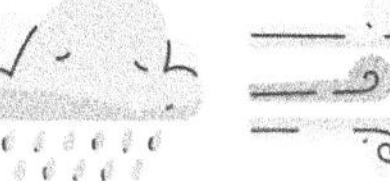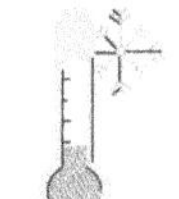

How many people?

What is your favourite type of flower?

Do you think each petal or leaf of a flower is exactly the same? Why/why not?

If you were abused, would you rather sleep in a flower or sleep on a leaf?

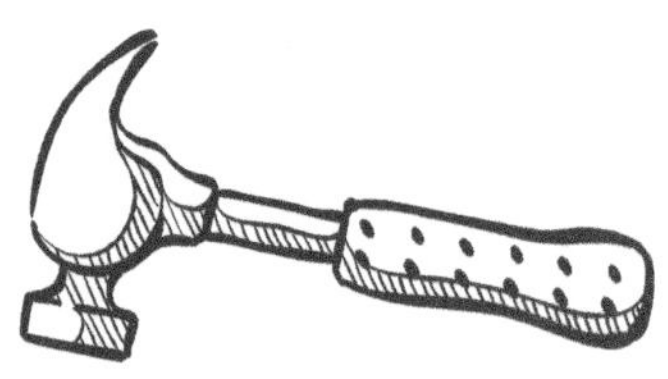 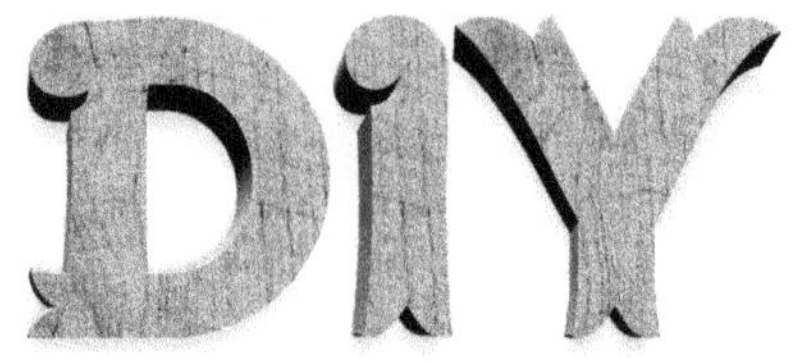

# DIY

Write your own challenge:

Date:                    Location:

Today's weather 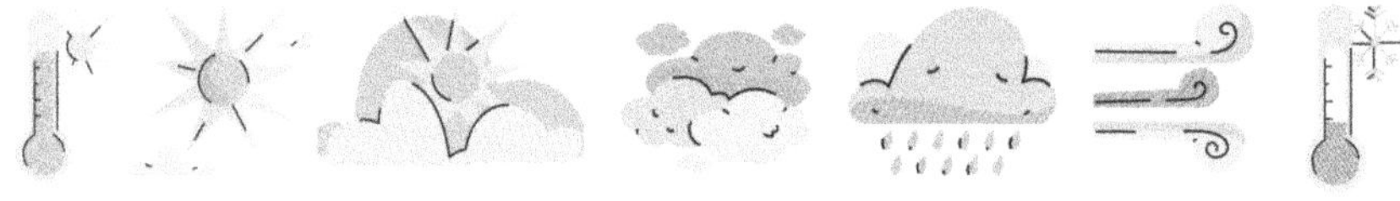

How many people? 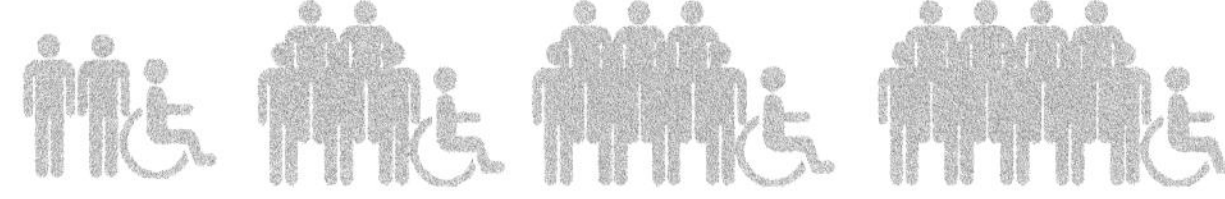

Who do you like to play with at school?

What is your favourite thing to do at school?

Where do you like to play at recess or lunch?

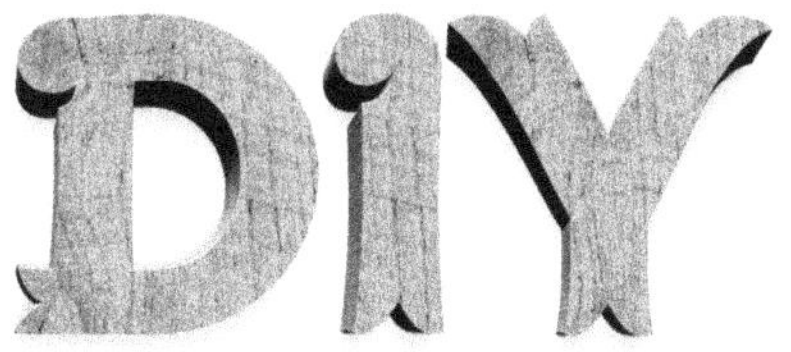


Write your own challenge:

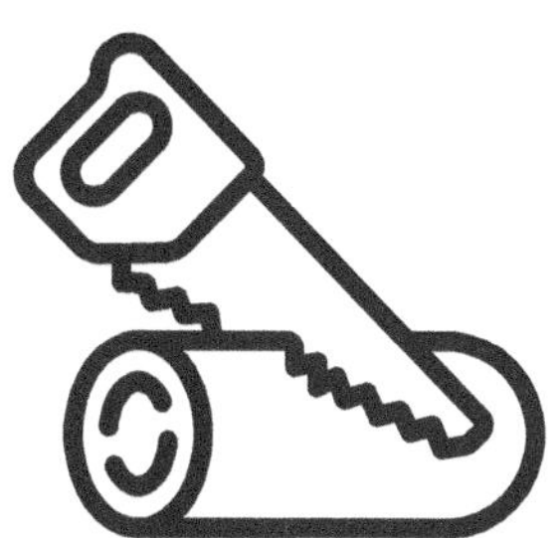

Date:                      Location:

Today's
 weather
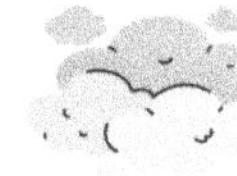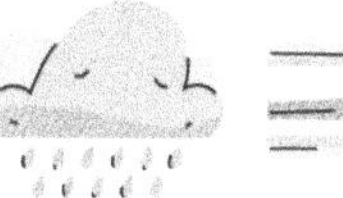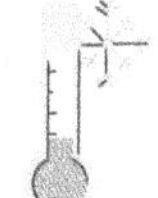

How many
people?
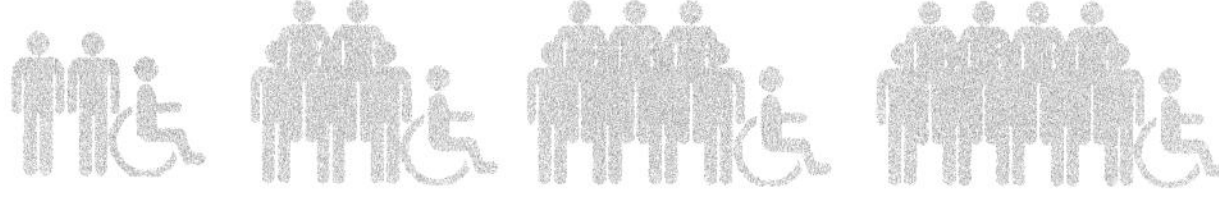

Where is your favourite place to go with your family?


When you go on holiday, what do you like to bring with you?


If you could choose anywhere in the world to go, where would you go for a
holiday?

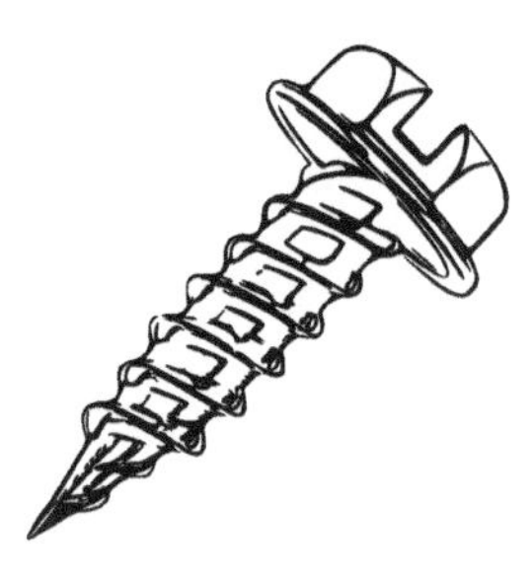

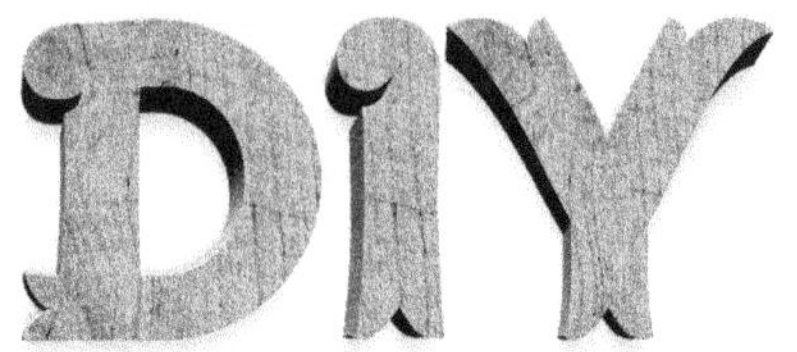


Write your own challenge:

Date:                        Location:

Today's
weather
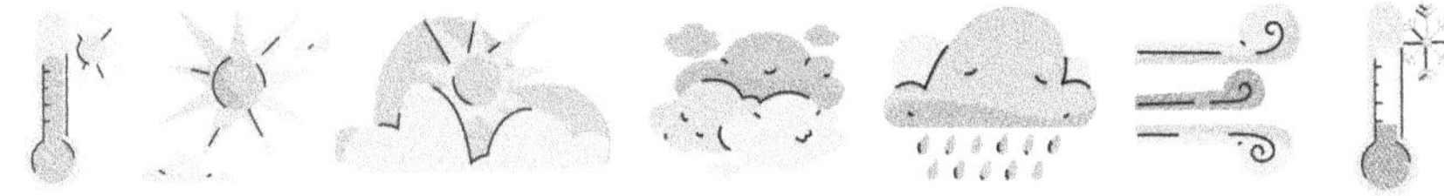

How many
people?
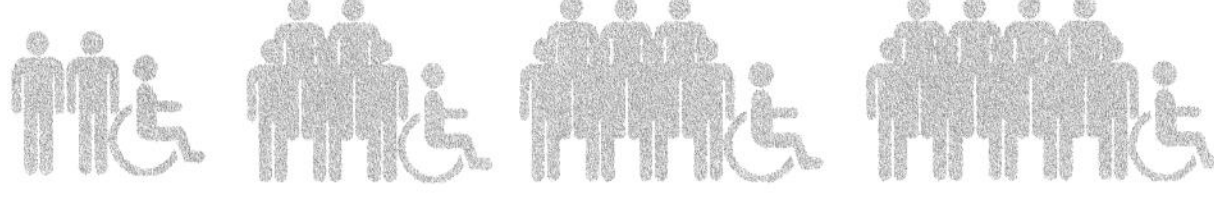

What is your favourite activity to do inside?


Which is your favourite toy to play with? Why?


When you want to relax and have a break, what do you like to do?

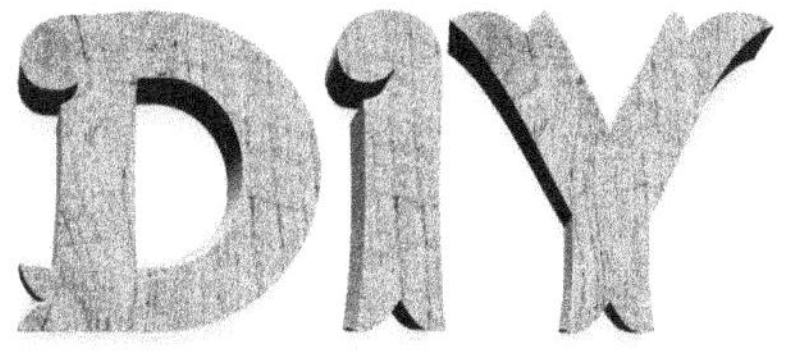


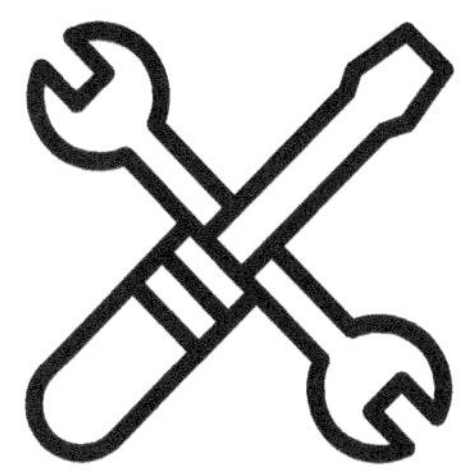

Write your own challenge:

Date:                    Location:

Today's
 weather

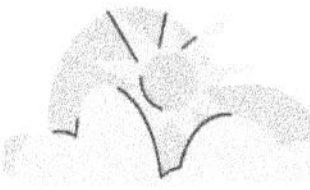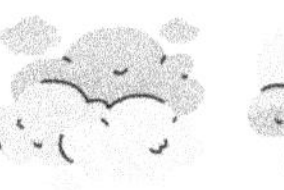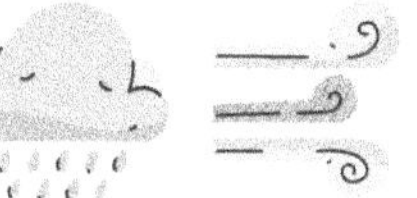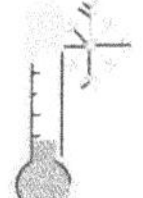

How many
people?

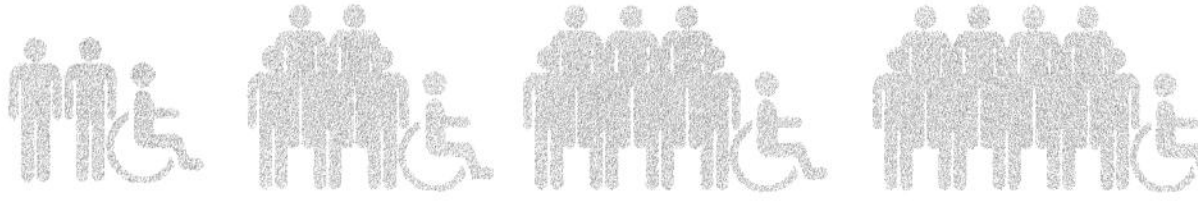

Where is your favourite place to play outside?

If you could do any activity outside, what would you choose to do?

Would you rather spend your time inside or outside of your house? Why?

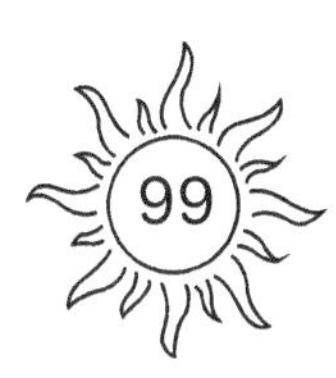

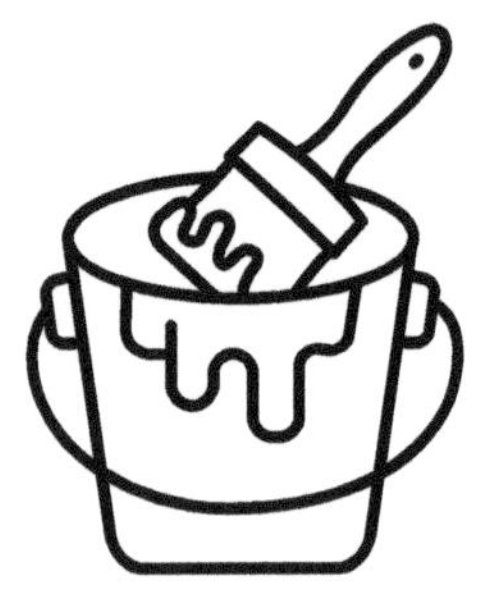

# 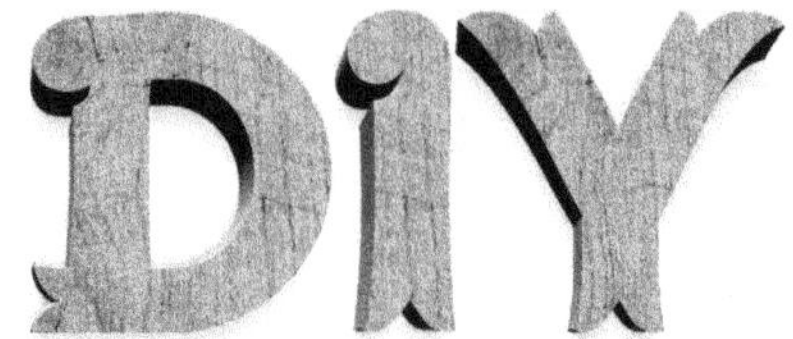DIY

Write your own challenge:

Date:                     Location:

Today's
weather 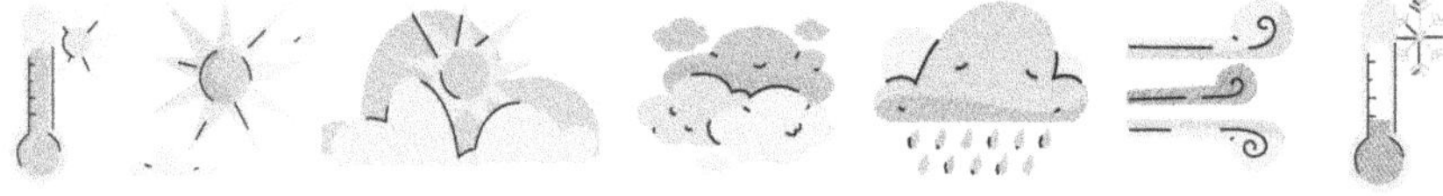

How many
people? 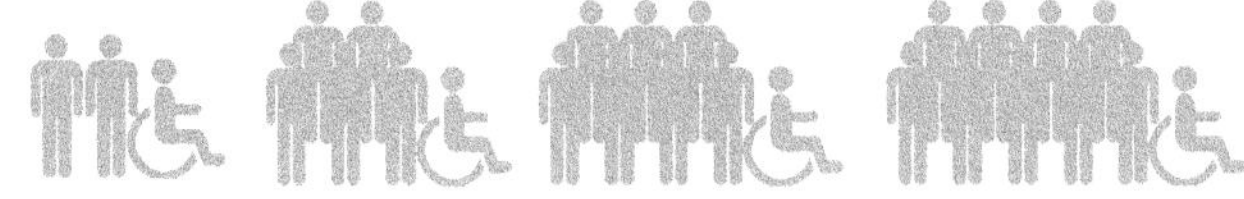

If you could be any movie character, who would you be?


Who is your favourite book character?


When you grow up, which character do you want to be the most like?

# MAKING MEMORIES